Welcome...

Are you running out the door without having eaten breakfast in the morning because you haven't had time to prep? Getting a takeaway because you've had a long day and don't feel like cooking? Are you putting off having friends over because you don't want to spend hours slaving away over the stove? Your slow cooker will not only save you time spent in the kitchen and make life easier, but it can also help you save money, energy and create healthier, delicious meals. From breakfasts and lighter meals to hearty mains, tempting bakes and desserts, we've got over 100 recipes for you to try so you can stress less and enjoy good food more. Let's get cooking!

Disclaimer
All the recipes in this book have been tested in a slow cooker; however some of the images are oven-baked as recipes can be made in both. Recipes may also vary depending on the make, size and shape of your slow cooker.

CONTENTS

Breakfasts

- 10 Scrambled eggs and salmon bagels
- 11 Smoky cheese soufflé omelette
- 11 French toast
- 12 Winter bircher muesli with a quick warming compote
- 12 Spicy Turkish eggs with sesame yoghurt
- 14 Spinach, olive and feta frittata
- 15 Classic kedgeree
- 15 Banana porridge oats

Lighter Meals

- 18 Curried parsnip soup
- 19 Chilli chicken nachos
- 21 Chicken, barley and vegetable soup
- 21 Mexican black bean and tomato soup
- 22 Spanish-style beans on jacket potato
- 22 Butternut and white bean soup with crispy parma ham
- 25 The full monty pizza
- 25 Minestrone soup
- 26 Japanese-style broth with udon noodles
- 26 Pulled jackfruit hoisin pancakes

p6 Slow cooker tips to save money and time.

Main Meals

Vegetarian

- 30 Saag aloo
- 30 Macaroni cheese
- 31 Moroccan lentil stew
- 33 Mascarpone and mushroom risotto with lemon and chive butter
- 33 Summer veg and harissa stew
- 34 Black bean quesadillas with avocado and salsa
- 36 Chilli vegetable hotpot
- 36 Fruity chickpea tagine
- 37 Vegan laksa
- 38 Butternut squash and sweetcorn korma
- 38 Black bean and roast sweet potato chilli with smoky sour cream
- 41 Aubergine caponata pasta
- 41 Ratatouille stew with herbed dumplings

Poultry

- 43 Chicken teriyaki rice bowl
- 44 Chicken giouvetsi (orzo chicken pasta)
- 44 Chicken and chorizo paella
- 46 Roast chicken with lemon and herbs
- 47 Super easy chicken curry
- 48 Creamy cider chicken casserole
- 48 Summer slow cooker cheesy chicken bake
- 50 Moroccan chicken tagine
- 53 Chipotle pulled chicken with slaw
- 53 North African chicken
- 54 Chinese five-spice chicken with sweetcorn
- 54 Chicken pilaf-style rice
- 56 Lighter chicken Milanese
- 57 Lemongrass and ginger chicken
- 59 Coq au champagne
- 60 Bombay braised chicken
- 60 Spicy prawn and chicken jambalaya
- 62 Turkey, butternut squash and coconut curry
- 63 Chicken korma
- 64 Chicken meatballs in red veg sauce with fettuccine
- 64 Chicken Thai red curry
- 66 Chicken cacciatore
- 69 Thai-style turkey and noodle soup
- 69 Chicken and vegetable stew

4 The Ultimate Slow Cooker Cookbook

37

80

128

Lamb
- 70 Italian lamb shank stew
- 71 Harissa lamb and feta pasta shells
- 72 Persian-style lamb stew
- 73 Spicy lamb meatballs in sherry sauce
- 75 Slow-roasted Provençale lamb
- 76 Spring lamb stew
- 77 Lamb with peppers, dates and chickpeas
- 78 Minty lamb and feta pasties
- 79 Spiced lamb tagine
- 79 Lamb pittas

Pork
- 80 Surprise sausage bolognese
- 80 Sweet miso pork
- 82 Pork with Bramley apple and tarragon
- 83 Slow-braised spicy pork and prunes
- 84 Pork chops with tomato and fennel sauce
- 86 Pulled pork
- 86 Chinese spiced pork belly with plums
- 89 Smoky pork and Boston beans one pot
- 89 Slow winter cottage pie
- 91 Spring pork and cider casserole

Beef
- 92 Ropa vieja
- 92 Beef chilli and black beans
- 94 Pulled beef ragu
- 95 Pot roast beef brisket
- 97 Steak fajitas
- 98 Beef short rib and leek hotpot
- 98 Beef rogan josh
- 100 Chiang Mai beef curry
- 101 Rich beef rendang
- 102 Speedy beef bourguignon
- 105 Beef curry with coconut chutney
- 105 Beef and sweet potato stew
- 107 Spanish oxtail stew with chorizo

Seafood
- 108 Spanish-style squid
- 108 Prawn and squash curry
- 111 Cod, chorizo and butter beans one-pan
- 112 French moules marinière
- 113 Salmon Provençale with freekeh

Game
- 115 Venison and butternut squash stew
- 115 Creamy cider rabbit stew
- 116 Crispy duck cassoulet

Desserts & Bakes
- 120 Guinness sticky toffee pudding
- 121 Poached pears with warm chocolate sauce
- 122 Cinnamon baked apples
- 122 Caramelised clementine risotto
- 123 Orange fairy cakes
- 124 Raspberry and coconut ice cream
- 125 Pineapple upside down cake
- 126 Banana bread
- 128 Change the mood chocolate pots
- 128 Brownies

TOP 10 SLOW COOKER TIPS

TOP 10 SLOW COOKER TIPS

Make the most out of your slow cooker! Save time and money with these simple tips

1 PREPARE THE NIGHT BEFORE

If you are using your slow cooker to save time, then consider prepping everything the night before, so that in the morning you just need to turn the slow cooker on. Prepare all of the ingredients and pop them into the slow cooker dish, cover and store it in the fridge overnight. When you wake up, take the dish out of the fridge to bring it up to room temperature. After half an hour or so, turn the cooker on.

2 SAVE MONEY WITH 'CHEAP' CUTS

Cooking meats slowly will tenderise them, which means using cheaper cuts of meat, that are often tougher, is perfect for a slow cooker. Use chicken thighs, beef brisket and pork shoulder. Cooking the meat slowly also enhances the meaty flavour, so you can use less meat than you might usually. Bulk your dishes up with vegetables instead.

3 TRIM THE FAT

When using a slow cooker you don't usually need to use oil, and you don't need the fat either. You can usually drain fat away when cooking the meat, but you can't necessarily do that with a slow cooker, so you are best to trim off any excess fat for a healthier, less fatty meal.

4 USE LESS LIQUID

Your slow cooker will seal in all of the moisture that you put into a dish, and the liquid won't evaporate like it would if you were cooking with a pot on the stove, so if you are using a recipe adapted for a slow cooker, use less liquid than suggested unless the recipe has no or little liquid or sauce in which case you'll need to add some.

5 USE FLOUR OR CORNFLOUR

You might have to use a thickening agent on some recipes if they come out very liquid. Either coat your meat in a little seasoned flour before cooking or wait until the dish is almost cooked and use cornflour. Add 1 or 2 tablespoons to a small amount of cold water and mix then add it carefully to your dish a little at a time, stirring as you do. Be careful you don't add too much as it won't immediately thicken – go a little at a time and leave for a minute or two.

TOP 10 SLOW COOKER TIPS

6 GO LOW
If you can, always use the low setting. This means you can switch it on and leave it all day without worrying about it too much. Low and slow will also mean the flavours will infuse and develop a lot better than if you cooked it faster.

7 LET IT DO ITS THING
Stop touching it! Slow cooker recipes are designed to be left alone. You shouldn't be lifting the lid and stirring it during the process. If you keep opening the lid you'll lose the heat that has built up inside but also you are defeating the purpose of using a slow cooker in order to free up your time to do other things.

8 ADD ALL OF THE INGREDIENTS AT THE START
It's likely you are choosing to cook with a slow cooker in order to save time and have more time for other things, so ideally you'll want to choose recipes that don't need much work while it cooks. Choose recipes that you can add all of the ingredients to at the very beginning and not have to touch again until it is time to serve.

9 KEEP PREP TIME TO A MINIMUM
Make sure you choose recipes that involve minimal preparation time, otherwise it sort of defeats the purpose of using a slow cooker to give you time away from standing over a stove. On the whole, most ingredients can just be thrown in together. Some recipes might call for you softening the onions first or browning the meat but in all honesty this isn't always essential. On days you have more time, perhaps experiment with this. You might find that the extra step of browning the meat adds nothing to your finished dish.

10 ADAPT YOUR RECIPES FOR A SLOW COOKER
You don't have to just use slow cooker specific recipes in your slow cooker, however, you will have to adapt the timings on a regular recipe. Obviously not everything can be cooked in a slow cooker, but if it has a sauce then chances are it will work. If the dish usually takes 15-30 minutes then cook it in the slow cooker for 1-2 hours on high and 4-6 hours on low. If it usually takes an hour then you probably need to cook it for 2-3 hours on high and 5-7 hours on low.

Think before you buy!
When buying a slow cooker, think about how many you will be cooking for. There is no point buying a massive one if you'll just be cooking for 2.

BREAKFASTS

BREAKFASTS

10	Scrambled eggs and salmon bagels	12	Spicy Turkish eggs with sesame yoghurt
11	Smoky cheese soufflé omelette	14	Spinach, olive and feta frittata
11	French toast	15	Classic kedgeree
12	Winter bircher muesli with a quick warming compote	15	Banana porridge oats

BREAKFASTS

*p*15
Porridge ready for you when you wake up!

BREAKFASTS

Scrambled eggs and salmon bagels

The perfect meal for when you're feeding a crowd brunch

Serves 4 • Ready in 2 hrs

- 4 wholegrain bagels, halved horizontally
- Good knob of butter
- 6 eggs, lightly beaten
- 8 slices smoked salmon
- Juice of ½ lemon
- 1tbsp dill, roughly chopped

1 Grease a slow cooker with butter.
2 Add the beaten eggs and season with salt and freshly ground black pepper. Cook the eggs on low for 2 hrs, stirring gently every 20 mins.
2 Toast the bagels. Divide the scrambled eggs between each bagel half, top with 2 slices of smoked salmon. Squeeze over a little lemon juice, add some black pepper and the dill. Top with the remaining bagel half and serve.

Cook's Tip
Try smoked trout, which is also high in omega-3s and cheaper than smoked salmon.

BREAKFASTS

Smoky cheese soufflé omelette

Using strongly flavoured cheese means you can reduce the quantity you use

Serves 2 • Ready in 50 mins

- 3 eggs, separated
- 1tbsp milk
- Good knob of butter
- Small handful of chopped flat-leaf parsley
- 100g (4oz) smoked Cheddar, coarsely grated

1 Grease a slow cooker with the butter.
2 In a medium bowl, whisk the egg whites to soft peaks. In another bowl, whisk the egg yolks with the milk, and season well with salt and freshly ground black pepper. Add about a quarter of the egg whites to the yolk mixture and stir in, then fold in the rest of the whites.
2 Add the omelette mixture and cook on high for 40 mins, until lightly set.
3 Sprinkle the parsley and cheese over one side. Switch off the slow cooker and leave for 10 mins letting the cheese melt a bit. Loosen the edges of the omelette with a palette knife, then fold it over and gently lift it out of slow cooker. Cut in half for serving, perhaps with grilled tomatoes and wilted spinach.

French toast

This is high in fibre and protein, but still a delicious sweet breakfast

Serves 2 • Ready in 1.5-3 hrs

- 2 eggs
- 1tbsp coconut milk
- 2tsp ground cinnamon
- 2 slices of flourless sprouted-grain bread, gluten-free bread or any thick sliced bread
- 1tsp extra-virgin coconut oil, for greasing
- 245ml (8.5fl oz) yoghurt
- 2tbsp pure maple syrup, rice syrup or coconut nectar
- Fresh fruit, to serve

1 Grease the slow cooker with the coconut oil.
2 Crack the eggs into a medium-size bowl and beat with a wire whisk. Add the coconut milk and cinnamon. Whisk again to mix.
3 Cut the slices of bread in half, making 4 halves. Put the bread into the slow cooker and pour over the egg mixture. Turn the bread over to make sure it's fully coated.
4 Cook on high for 1.5 hrs or on low for 3 hrs and then carefully lift on to a plate.
5 While the French toast is cooking, whisk the yoghurt and syrup together in a small bowl. Top the French toast with dollops of the yoghurt. Alternatively, dust with powdered sugar. Serve with fresh fruit.

BREAKFASTS

Winter Bircher muesli with a quick warming compote

This easy brunch can be prepped the night before, involves minimal work and is full of goodness and warmth

Serves 4 • Ready in 2 hrs, plus overnight chilling

For the muesli
- 200g (7oz) oats
- 500ml (17fl oz) oat milk
- 1tsp cinnamon
- ½tsp vanilla bean paste
- 50g (2oz) hazelnuts, roughly chopped
- 50g (2oz) pecans, roughly chopped
- 1 apple, grated
- 300ml (10fl oz) apple juice
- 2tbsp chia seeds

For the compote
- 2 pears, peeled and deseeded
- 1 clementine
- 100ml (3.5fl oz) cloudy apple juice

1 Mix the oats, oat milk, cinnamon, vanilla bean paste, apple, apple juice and chia seeds in the slow cooker. Cover and cook on low until the liquid has absorbed (about 2 hrs).
2 In a medium pan, chop the pears into chunks, grate in the zest of the clementine, and peel and chop the clementine fruit. Add the apple juice; heat over a medium heat for 5-10 mins or until broken down.
3 When ready to serve, warm through if eating hot, adjust the sweetness and add a little extra milk if needed.
4 Serve with the fruit compote and a little natural yoghurt on the side, if you like.

Spicy Turkish eggs with sesame yoghurt

This delicious Turkish dish is perfect for breakfast or brunch

Serves 4 • Ready in 4 hrs 20 mins

- 3tbsp olive oil
- 2 large onions, thinly sliced
- 1 red, 1 green and 1 yellow pepper, each cut into round slices
- 3 garlic cloves, finely chopped
- ½tsp each cumin seeds, caraway seeds and cayenne pepper
- 1tbsp tomato purée
- 400g (14oz) tin chopped tomatoes
- A few cherry tomatoes, pierced
- 1 bunch of flat-leaf parsley
- 80g (3oz) spinach, wilted
- 1tsp harissa (optional)
- 3-4 eggs
- 80g (3oz) feta, crumbled
- 2 spring onions, chopped
- 250g (9oz) thick natural yoghurt
- 4 heaped tsp tahini
- Pitta breads and olives, to serve

1 Heat the oil in a large frying pan. Add the onions and peppers, and season. Cook for 3 mins. Add the garlic and cook for a further 1 min.
2 Place the onion mixture into the slow cooker with the cumin, caraway seeds and cayenne pepper. Stir in the tomato purée and tomatoes.
4 Add 60ml (2.5fl oz) water. Cover and cook on low for 3-4 hrs.
5 Stir in chopped parsley, spinach and harissa (if you want it spicier).
6 Increase heat to high. Make 3-4 indentations. Break an egg into a cup and drop carefully into each dip. Cover and cook on high until the whites are set and the yolks are to your liking (about 20 mins for slightly runny yolks).
7 Sprinkle over the feta and spring onions. Serve with yoghurt and tahini mixed together on the side, plus pitta breads and olives.

BREAKFASTS

BREAKFASTS

Spinach, olive and feta frittata

Leftover frittata is perfect for packed lunches

Serves 6 • Ready in 4 hrs

- 1tbsp light olive oil
- 1 red onion, sliced finely
- 1tsp caster sugar
- 80g (3oz) bag baby spinach
- 200g (7oz) pack feta cheese, roughly cubed
- 50g (2oz) black olives, pitted and halved
- 6 large eggs, beaten
- 1tbsp butter, to grease

1 Grease the slow cooker well with the butter.
2 Heat the oil in a frying pan, add the onion and sugar, and cook over a medium heat for 5-7 mins. Turn off the heat and add the spinach until it wilts. Spoon into the slow cooker.
3 Add the feta and olives and stir to mix up slightly. Season the beaten eggs well with salt and pepper and then pour over the vegetables.
4 Cook for 4 hrs on low or until just set in the centre. Leave to cool for 5 mins. Carefully remove from slow cooker and cool completely on a wire wrack. Serve cut into wedges.

Cook's Tip
Halloumi cheese would also work but as it's very salty, only season your frittata with pepper.

BREAKFASTS

Classic kedgeree

Typically a breakfast dish, but this makes a great speedy supper too

Serves 4 • Ready in 2 hrs

- 500g (1lb) undyed smoked haddock
- ½tsp dried chilli flakes
- 400ml (14fl oz) milk
- 2tbsp vegetable oil
- 2 medium onions, chopped
- 300g (10.5oz) basmati rice
- 1tbsp medium curry powder
- 3 cardamom pods, split
- ½tsp turmeric
- 1 cinnamon stick, broken in half
- 500ml (17fl oz) gluten-free vegetable stock
- 250ml (9fl oz) boiling water
- 3 free-range hard-boiled eggs, peeled and quartered
- 175g (6oz) cooked peas
- A handful of coriander leaves, and lime wedges, to serve

1 Place the haddock, chilli flakes and milk in a pan. Bring to the boil, then reduce the heat and simmer for 5 mins.
2 Meanwhile, heat the oil in a large frying pan and cook the onions for 5 mins until soft. Add the rice, curry powder, cardamom, turmeric and cinnamon to the pan, and stir to combine. Then remove the cinnamon sticks.
3 Place the rice mixture into the slow cooker. Flake the fish and add to the slow cooker along with 500ml (17fl oz) vegetable stock and 250ml (9fl oz) of boiling water. Stir well, cover and cook on high for 1.5 to 2 hrs.
4 When ready to serve, add the quartered eggs and peas and fold through gently until heated through.
5 Season to taste. Scatter over the coriander and serve with the lime wedges.

Banana porridge oats

You can't beat a perfect porridge that keeps you full 'till lunch

Serves 4 • Ready in 7-8 hrs

- 1tbsp salted butter
- 150g (5oz) jumbo rolled oats
- 400ml (14fl oz) milk
- 750ml (25fl oz) water
- 4tbsp runny honey
- 2 bananas, sliced

1 Grease a slow cooker with butter to prevent the oats from sticking.
2 Combine the oats, milk and water in the slow cooker and stir. Place the lid on, and leave overnight on low for 7-8 hrs.
3 In the morning, stir and loosen with a splash of milk, if needed. Serve with 1tbsp of honey per bowl, and topped with banana.

The Ultimate Slow Cooker Cookbook **15**

LIGHTER MEALS

p22
Slow cooker soups ready before lunch!

LIGHTER MEALS

18 Curried parsnip soup	22 Butternut and white bean soup with crispy parma ham
19 Chilli chicken nachos	25 The full monty pizza
21 Chicken, barley and vegetable soup	25 Minestrone soup
21 Mexican black bean and tomato soup	26 Japanese-style broth with udon noodles
22 Spanish-style beans on jacket potato	26 Pulled jackfruit hoisin pancakes

LIGHTER MEALS

Curried parsnip soup

The delicious naan croutons make this tasty soup something extra special. For a vegan version, omit the cream and croutons

Serves 4 • Ready in 3-6 hrs

- 2tsp olive oil
- 1 onion, chopped
- 1 garlic clove, crushed
- 1tbsp garam masala
- ½tsp turmeric
- ¼tsp mustard powder
- ¼tsp ground cinnamon
- Pinch cayenne pepper, plus extra to serve (optional)
- 500g (1lb 10oz) parsnips, peeled and chopped
- 1 large potato, chopped
- 1l (1.75pt) vegetable stock
- 1 naan bread
- ¼tsp nigella seeds (optional)
- 70ml (2.5fl oz) double cream, plus extra to serve (optional)
- Coriander leaves, to serve (optional)

1 Heat half the oil in a saucepan and add the onion. Cook over medium heat until soft and translucent. Add the garlic and spices and cook for 1 min. Add the mixture along with the parsnips, potato and stock to the slow cooker. Cook on high for 3 hrs or on low for 6 hrs.

2 Meanwhile, heat the oven to 180°C/350°F/Gas 4. Cut the naan into cubes and toss with the remaining 1tsp of oil, and the nigella seeds. Scatter in a single layer over a baking tray and cook for 10-15 mins until golden. These are your naan croutons.

3 Use a stick blend to purée the soup in the slow cooker until smooth. Stir in the cream then serve with an extra sprinkling of cayenne, and the coriander and naan croutons.

4 If making ahead, freeze for up to 3 months (or it will keep in the fridge for a couple of days), defrost completely and reheat on the hob. If freezing the croutons, defrost them completely. Place in a hot oven for 5 mins with a little more oil to re-crisp.

LIGHTER MEALS

Chilli chicken nachos

Easy to scale up if you're serving a crowd, this relaxed supper is a sure-fire winner!

Serves 4 • Ready in 6-8 hrs

For the chicken:
- 4-5 chicken breasts
- 1 onion, coarsely chopped
- 3 garlic cloves, chopped
- 1.25l (2.5pt) water (or enough to cover chicken depending on pot)

For the seasoning:
- 1tbsp chilli powder
- 2tbsp paprika
- 2tbsp cumin
- 2tbsp salt
- 1tsp ground cayenne pepper
- 3 whole dried chipotle peppers

For the nachos:
- 200g (7oz) bag salted tortilla chips
- 400g (14oz) can black beans
- 200g (7oz) tub fresh tomato salsa
- 150ml (5fl oz) soured cream
- 300g (10.5oz) grated Cheddar
- 4tbsp pickled sliced jalapeños
- 2 avocado, stoned and diced
- Fresh coriander leaves, to serve

1 Add the onions, garlic, chicken, seasoning and water to the slow cooker and cook on low for 6-8 hrs. Once cooked, shred the chicken using two forks.
2 Preheat the oven to 190°C/375°F/Gas 5. Layer the tortilla chips, black beans, chicken, salsa, soured cream and most of the Cheddar into an ovenproof dish (use individual dishes if you can want so you can serve straight out of the oven).
2 Cover the tin with foil and bake for 20 mins until warmed through.
3 Sprinkle over the remaining Cheddar and jalapeños and finish off under the grill for a further 5-10 mins, until the cheese has melted and the tips of the nachos are crispy.
4 Scatter over the diced avocado and coriander leaves. Serve warm.

LIGHTER MEALS

Chicken, barley and vegetable soup

This is great for using up any leftover roast chicken. Feel free to use any vegetables you have

Serves 6 • Ready in 3-6 hrs

- 400ml (14fl oz) chicken stock
- 1 large onion, peeled and finely chopped
- 2 small bay leaves and a few sprigs of thyme or rosemary
- 1kg (2lb) mixed winter veg – we used carrot, turnip, swede, celeriac and parsnip
- 2 sticks of celery
- 100g (3.5oz) pearl barley
- 600g (1lb 5oz) cooked chicken, shredded
- Freshly chopped parsley, to garnish

1 Peel and chop all the vegetables, trim and chop the celery.
2 Put all the vegetables, onion and herbs in the slow cooker and pour over the stock. Cook on high for 2 hrs or on low for 4 hrs.
3 Add the barley and cook for another 1 hr on high or 2 hrs on low.
4 Shred the chicken and return to the pot. Season the soup and ladle it into bowls. Sprinkle with parsley and serve with chunks of bread.

> "Rice or bulgar wheat can be used if you don't have barley in the pantry"

LIGHTER MEALS

Mexican black bean & tomato soup

Spice up your lunch with this aromatic soup

Serves 6 • Ready in 2 hrs

- 1tbsp olive oil
- 1 onion, peeled and chopped
- 1 stick celery, chopped
- 1 carrot, chopped
- 1 red chilli, chopped
- 1tsp paprika
- 1tsp ground cumin
- 1tsp ground coriander
- 400g (14oz) can chopped tomatoes
- 600ml (20fl oz) stock
- 400g (14oz) can black beans

To serve
- 1 large avocado (175g/6oz)
- 2 tomatoes, chopped and tossed in lime
- 50g (2oz) corn tortillas, broken up
- 6tbsp natural yoghurt or half-fat soured cream
- Handful fresh coriander

1 Add all the soup ingredients to the pot, apart from the beans (add these for the last hr) and reduce the amount of stock to 200ml (7fl oz). Cook on high for 2 hrs.
2 Blitz with a stick blender, divide between six bowls and sprinkle with the toppings.

LIGHTER MEALS

Cook's Tip
For extra-crispy jacket skins: after step 2, place the unwrapped potatoes in the oven for 20-30 mins at 220°C/430°F/Gas 7.

Spanish-style beans on jacket potato

Switch regular baked beans for some tinned cannellini beans in a smoky, spiced tomato sauce

Serves 2 • Ready in 7-8 hrs

- 2 large baking potatoes
- 1 tsp olive oil
- Salt
- 1 small red onion, diced
- 1 red pepper, diced
- 1 garlic clove, crushed
- 1tsp smoked paprika
- 400g (14oz) cannellini beans, drained
- 150ml (5oz) passata
- Pinch of sugar
- Freshly ground black pepper
- 2tbsp crème fraîche
- Small handful parsley, chopped

1 Rinse, scrub and thoroughly dry the potatoes. Pierce the skins a few times with a fork, then rub them with olive oil and sprinkle with salt. Wrap each potato tightly with foil and set aside.
2 Add the onion, pepper, garlic, paprika, beans, passata and sugar to your slow cooker and stir. Place the foil-wrapped potatoes on top.
2 Cook on low for 7-8 hrs, until the potatoes are cooked through and the beans are tender. Remove the potatoes and carefully unwrap them to let any steam escape safely. Season the beans with salt and pepper to taste.
3 Split the potatoes and spoon in the saucy beans, then top with the crème fraîche and parsley.

Butternut and white bean soup with crispy Parma ham

This smooth, velvety soup is all the more special with a sprinkling of crispy Parma ham and a good grating of Parmesan

Serves 4 • Ready in 3-6 hrs

- 1 onion, chopped
- 1 large carrot, chopped
- 1 celery stalk, chopped
- 1 butternut squash, peeled, deseeded and chopped (about 800g/1lb 12oz)
- 100ml (3.5fl oz) dry white wine
- 750ml (1lb 10oz) chicken or vegetable stock
- 400g (14oz) tin cannellini beans, drained and rinsed
- 4 slices Parma ham
- 2tbsp freshly grated Parmesan
- Focaccia or ciabatta, to serve

1 Place your chopped onion, carrot, celery and butternut squash in the slow cooker. Add the white wine, chicken stock and cannellini beans and stir, before placing the lid on the slow cooker. Cook for 3 hrs on high, or 5-6 hrs on low.
2 Before serving, brush a large frying pan with a little oil and cook the ham over a high heat for 1-2 mins each side. Leave to cool and crisp, then break into small shards.
3 Using a stick blender, purée the soup until smooth. Check the seasoning then ladle into bowls and top with pepper, Parmesan and Parma ham, with the bread on the side.

LIGHTER MEALS

LIGHTER MEALS

Cook's Tip
To make your own peri-peri sprinkle mini chicken fillets with Nando's Peri-Peri Salt.

LIGHTER MEALS

The full monty pizza

Sometimes more really is more

Serves 4 • Ready in 2 hrs, plus the time it takes to make your base

For the base:
- 1tbsp caster sugar
- 250g (9oz) gluten-free strong bread flour
- 1tsp easy-bake yeast
- 1tsp sea salt
- 2tbsp polenta or cornmeal

For the topping:
- 300g (10.5oz) peri-peri chicken
- 1 red onion, chopped
- 1 yellow pepper, sliced
- 3tbsp olive oil
- 4tbsp red pepper and tomato salsa
- 100g (3.5oz) mozzarella, grated
- 60g (2.5oz) pepperoni
- 5 Peppadews (piquanté mild/sweet peppers), drained and chopped
- 1tbsp jalapeño peppers, chopped
- 8 black pitted olives
- Basil leaves

1 Heat the oven to 200°C/400°F/Gas 6. Place the chicken, onion and pepper in a large roasting tin. Drizzle with 2tbsp oil; cook for 15 mins.
2 Dissolve the sugar in 150ml (5fl oz) warm water. Mix the flour with the yeast and salt. Add the water mixture to this and mix into a dough. Knead until smooth. Set in an oiled bowl, cover with damp tea towel and leave to rise in a warm place for 20 mins.
3 Spritz slow cooker with cooking spray to grease, then spread the dough out on the bottom and 1cm (0.5in) up the sides. Sprinkle over polenta; leave to rise for 20 mins.
4 Spread the salsa over the base, and sprinkle on the mozzarella. Top with all the other ingredients. Cook on low for 2 hrs, until the crust is golden and the cheese has melted.

Minestrone soup

This is the ultimate warming winter soup — perfect for those chilly nights

Serves 4 • Ready in 3-7 hrs

- ½tbsp olive oil
- 1 onion, finely chopped
- 3 sticks celery, chopped
- 2 carrots, diced
- 1 small leek, halved vertically, washed and finely sliced
- 100g (3.5oz) cavolo nero, central stalks removed, leaves shredded
- 1tbsp tomato purée
- 400g (14oz) tin cannellini beans
- 400g (14oz) tin chopped tomatoes
- 800ml (27fl oz) hot chicken stock
- Sprig of rosemary
- 100g (3.5oz) conchigliette or vermicelli pasta
- 50g (2oz) Grana Padano cheese, finely grated, plus rind
- 100g (3.5oz) smoked lardons (optional)

1 Heat the oil in a pan over a low heat. If using lardons, cook for 10 mins and then add to the slow cooker.
2 In the same pan, add the chopped onion, celery, carrots and leek. Cook for 5 mins until the veg has softened.
3 Mix in the tomato purée and beans, then pour over the chopped tomatoes and stock. Bring to the boil, then transfer to the slow cooker. Add the rosemary, replace the lid and cook on high for 3-4 hrs, or 6-7 hrs on low.
4 Half an hour before serving, remove the slow cooker lid and add the pasta, cavolo nero and the cheese rind. Replace the lid and leave for 30 mins, or until the pasta is tender.
5 Season with salt and pepper, take out the rind and serve topped with the grated cheese.

LIGHTER MEALS

Cook's Tip
For a veggie option, leave out the meat, double the mushrooms and add more mangetout and nori seaweed.

Japanese-style broth with udon noodles

This warming and savoury Japanese style broth is filling and hearty, but still healthy

Serves 3-4 • Ready in 2 hrs

- 175g (6oz) dried udon noodles or use wholewheat noodles (3 nests)
- 1.5l (2.5pt) vegetable or beef stock (use 3 cubes)
- 5cm (2in) piece of fresh root ginger, sliced into thin slivers
- 1 sachet miso instant soup paste (or use frozen Thai herbs or some Thai green curry paste, to taste)
- 1-2tbsp fish sauce or soy sauce, to taste
- 1 red chilli, deseeded and thinly sliced
- 1 large clove garlic, thinly sliced
- 250g (9oz) mixed mushrooms – button, shiitake, oyster, thinly sliced or torn into bite-sized pieces
- 100g (3.5oz) mangetout, cut into fine strips
- 150g (5oz) finely sliced fillet steak
- 2 spring onions, trimmed and shredded, optional
- Lime wedges, to serve

1 Add the mushrooms, stock, ginger, miso paste, fish sauce, chilli and garlic to the slow cooker. Cook for 1.5 hrs on high.
2 Add the noodles and steak strips, if using (or extra firm tofu chunks if you want a veggie option). Cook for a further 30 mins. In the last 10 mins add in the mangetout.
3 Season to taste with more fish or soy sauce.
4 Divide the noodles between 3-4 warm bowls and spoon the hot broth over. Sprinkle over shredded spring onions, if using, and serve with lime wedges.

Pulled jackfruit hoisin pancakes

Pulled jackfruit has a texture that's quite meaty, and it makes a great substitute for duck or pulled pork

Serves 4 • Ready in 2 hrs

- 1 tin jackfruit in brine (we used Naked Jackfruit)
- 200ml (7fl oz) hoisin sauce
- 1 cucumber
- 3 spring onions
- 12 ready-made Chinese pancakes

1 Drain the tin of jackfruit and shred the pieces with 2 forks, or using your hands, until all the fruit is broken up. Add the shredded jackfruit and the hoisin sauce to the slow cooker, stir and cook for 2 hrs on high.
2 Meanwhile, cut the cucumber and spring onions into matchsticks. Once ready to serve, heat the pancakes in the microwave for 30 secs, or according to the pack instructions.
3 Serve the individual components separately and allow everyone to build their own pancakes by topping with shredded jackfruit and crunchy vegetable sticks.

"Rinse the tinned jackfruit in water to get rid of the sweet flavour"

LIGHTER MEALS

MAIN MEALS

p101
Tender meat with recipes like this beef curry.

MAIN MEALS

Vegetarian
- 30 Saag aloo
- 30 Macaroni cheese
- 31 Moroccan red lentil and vegetable stew
- 33 Mascarpone and mushroom risotto with lemon and chive butter
- 33 Summer veg and harissa stew
- 34 Black bean quesadillas with avocado and salsa
- 36 Chilli vegetable hotpot
- 36 Fruity chickpea tagine
- 37 Vegan laksa
- 38 Butternut squash and sweetcorn korma
- 38 Black bean and roast sweet potato chilli with smoky sour cream
- 41 Aubergine caponata pasta
- 41 Ratatouille stew with herbed dumplings

Poultry
- 43 Chicken teriyaki rice bowl
- 44 Chicken giouvetsi (orzo chicken pasta)
- 44 Chicken and chorizo paella
- 46 Roast chicken with lemon and herbs
- 47 Super easy chicken curry
- 48 Creamy cider chicken casserole
- 48 Summer slow cooker cheesy chicken bake
- 50 Moroccan chicken tagine
- 53 Chipotle pulled chicken with slaw
- 53 North African chicken
- 54 Chinese five-spice chicken with sweetcorn
- 54 Chicken pilaf-style rice
- 56 Lighter chicken Milanese
- 57 Lemongrass and ginger chicken
- 59 Coq au champagne
- 60 Bombay braised chicken
- 60 Spicy prawn and chicken jambalaya
- 62 Turkey, butternut squash and coconut curry
- 63 Chicken korma
- 64 Chicken meatballs in red veg sauce with fettuccine
- 64 Chicken Thai red curry
- 66 Chicken cacciatore
- 69 Thai-style turkey and noodle soup
- 69 Chicken and vegetable stew

Lamb
- 70 Italian lamb shank stew
- 71 Harissa lamb and feta pasta shells
- 72 Persian-style lamb stew
- 73 Spicy lamb meatballs in sherry sauce
- 75 Slow-roasted Provençale lamb
- 76 Spring lamb stew
- 77 Lamb with peppers, dates and chickpeas
- 78 Minty lamb and feta pasties
- 79 Spiced lamb tagine
- 79 Lamb pittas

Pork
- 80 Surprise sausage bolognese
- 80 Sweet miso pork
- 82 Pork with Bramley apple and tarragon
- 83 Slow-braised spicy pork and prunes
- 84 Pork chops with tomato and fennel sauce
- 86 Pulled pork
- 86 Chinese spiced pork belly with plums
- 89 Smoky pork and Boston beans one pot
- 89 Slow winter cottage pie
- 91 Spring pork and cider casserole

Beef
- 92 Ropa vieja
- 92 Beef chilli and black beans
- 94 Pulled beef ragu
- 95 Pot roast beef brisket
- 97 Steak fajitas
- 98 Beef short rib and leek hotpot
- 98 Beef rogan josh
- 100 Chiang Mai beef curry
- 101 Rich beef rendang
- 102 Speedy beef bourguignon
- 105 Beef curry with fresh coconut chutney
- 105 Beef and sweet potato stew
- 107 Spanish oxtail stew with chorizo

Seafood
- 108 Spanish-style squid
- 108 Prawn and squash curry
- 111 Cod, chorizo and butter beans one-pan
- 112 French moules marinière
- 113 Salmon Provençale with freekeh

Game
- 115 Venison and butternut squash stew
- 115 Creamy cider rabbit stew
- 116 Crispy duck cassoulet

MAIN MEALS

Saag aloo

You will probably have tried this at your local Indian so why not try and make it at home and save the cals and the cost

Serves 4 • Ready in 1 hr 10 mins

- 2tbsp vegetable oil
- 1 onion, peeled and sliced
- 1 garlic clove, puréed
- 1 red chilli, deseeded and sliced
- 1tbsp fresh ginger, peeled and grated
- 1tsp black mustard seeds
- 1tsp cumin seeds
- 1tsp turmeric
- 500g (1lb) potatoes, cut into chunks and parboiled
- 200g (7oz) spinach
- 50ml (2fl oz) water

1 Switch the slow cooker on to low. Heat the oil in a pan, add the onion and cook on a low heat for 5 mins to soften.
2 Add the garlic, chilli, ginger and spices and cook for a further 3 mins.
3 Add the parboiled potatoes to the slow cooker with the spinach and ingredients from steps 1 and 2.
4 Season with salt and pepper. Stir and cook for 1 hr on low. Serve with rice and naan bread or as a side.

Macaroni cheese

A warming and nourishing pot of pasta with a cheesy sauce to fill you with joy

Serves 4 • Ready in 1 hr 50 mins

- 1.75l (3pt) milk
- 450g (1lb) macaroni, or other pasta
- 115g (4oz) butter
- 250g (9oz) grated cheddar cheese
- 1tsp mustard powder (optional)

1 Add all of the ingredients to the slow cooker, saving enough cheese to sprinkle on top of the dish later. Mix well and cook on high for 1 hr 45 mins, stirring once or twice during cooking.
2 Season with salt and pepper. Fold the sauce through the pasta until it has combined to make a creamy coating.
3 Pour into an ovenproof dish. Sprinkle the remaining cheese in a thin layer on top of the pasta and place under a hot grill. When the cheese begins to brown remove the dish from the grill.
5 Serve immediately either on its own or as an accompaniment to a larger meal.

MAIN MEALS

Moroccan red lentil and vegetable stew

Exotic spices give this its authentic flavour and lentils are so nutritious too

Serves 4 • Ready in 3.5-6 hrs

- 2tbsp olive oil
- 1 onion, peeled and sliced
- 1 garlic clove, peeled and chopped
- 1tsp each paprika, turmeric and cumin
- ¼tsp each cinnamon and ground ginger
- 1tbsp tomato purée
- 3 medium potatoes, peeled and cut into 2.5cm (1in) cubes
- 300g (10oz) butternut squash, peeled, deseeded and cubed
- 125g (4.5oz) red lentils
- 400g (14oz) chopped tomatoes
- 400ml (13.5fl oz) hot vegetable stock
- 2tsp vegetarian yeast extract (such as marmite)
- 1tsp runny honey
- Handful fresh coriander leaves

1 Heat the oil in a frying pan. Add the onion and garlic to the pan and cook for 5 mins until softened.
2 Add the onion mixture (replace with 1tsp of garlic to skip step 1), spices, tomato purée, potatoes, squash, lentils, tomatoes, hot stock, yeast extract and honey to the slow cooker. Season with salt. Cover and cook for 3.5 hrs on high or 6 hrs on low, until the vegetables are very tender. Serve, sprinkled with coriander.

MAIN MEALS

Mushroom and mascarpone risotto with lemon and chive butter

We stir in mascarpone at the end of the cooking to give the rice a soft, creamier texture

Serves 4 • Ready in 2 hrs

- 15g (0.5oz) dried porcini mushrooms
- 50g (2oz) unsalted butter, softened
- Finely grated zest 1 lemon
- 2tbsp finely chopped chives
- 2tbsp olive oil
- 1 small onion, finely chopped
- 300g (10.5oz) mixed mushrooms, sliced
- Vegetable stock pot or cube
- 300g (10.5oz) Arborio risotto rice
- 150ml (5fl oz) dried white wine
- 150g (5oz) mascarpone
- 50g (2oz) Parmesan, freshly grated, plus, extra to serve
- 250ml (9fl oz) warm water

1 Put the dried mushrooms in a heatproof jug, pour in 600ml (20fl oz) boiling water and leave to soak for 30 mins.
2 Meanwhile, beat the butter until very soft then mix in the lemon zest and chives. Spoon the butter onto a rectangle of baking paper and roll up into a cylinder, twisting the ends to seal. Put in the fridge for 20 mins.
3 Heat the oil in a frying pan and cook the onion for 5 mins. Add the mixed mushrooms and cook a further 5 mins.
4 Strain the mushroom-soaking liquid into a saucepan and add the stock pot. Bring to a low simmer. Chop the soaked mushrooms.
5 Add the rice to the saucepan, stirring to coat in the oil. Add the wine and bubble vigorously for 2-3 mins. Stir in the dried mushrooms and half the stock. Pour into the slow cooker.
6 Add the remainder of the stock and 250ml (9fl oz) warm water. Cook for 30 mins on high or 1 hr on low.
7 Once cooked, stir in the Parmesan and mascarpone, and season.
8 Serve the risotto topped with a disc of butter and sprinkle of Parmesan.

MAIN MEALS

Cook's Tip
To give the dish some extra flavour, you can roast some of the veg in the oven for 15-20 mins before step 2.

Summer veg and harissa stew

A spring take on a hearty veggie one-pot, harissa adds a rich smokiness

Serves 4-6 • Ready in 3-6 hrs

For the stew:
- 2 x 400g (14oz) tins chopped tomatoes
- 1 x vegetable stock cube, dissolved in 2-3tbsp freshly boiled water
- 2 x 400g (14oz) tins chickpeas (or cannellini or butter beans)
- 1 large aubergine, chopped
- 1 red pepper, sliced
- 1tbsp olive oil
- 1 red onion, sliced
- 2 garlic cloves, crushed
- 2 large courgettes, chopped
- 2-4tbsp harissa, to taste
- 1tbsp tomato purée
- 1tsp cumin

To serve:
- Large bunch parsley or dill, chopped
- Flatbreads
- Greek yoghurt or a vegan alternative
- Harissa (optional)

1 If you prefer a thicker stew, drain some of the liquid from the chopped tomato tins. Discard the excess liquid, or save it for another stew or soup.
2 Add all the ingredients for the stew to the bowl of your slow cooker and mix everything together. Cook for 3-4 hrs on high, or 5-6 hrs on low.
3 Once the stew is done, stir in half the parsley and serve with flatbreads, a dollop of yoghurt, scatter with remaining parsley, and drizzle with extra harissa if desired.

MAIN MEALS

Black bean quesadillas with avocado and salsa

A great veggie weeknight option. The quesadilla is filling, so would easily serve 3-4 with more salad

Serves 2 • Ready in 2 hrs 30 mins

- 400g (14oz) tin black beans, drained
- 50g (2oz) tinned sweetcorn, drained
- ¼tsp chilli flakes
- 1tsp smoked paprika
- 3 spring onions, thinly sliced
- 150g (5oz) Wensleydale or other crumbly cheese, grated
- Bunch coriander, finely chopped
- 2 large flour tortillas
- To serve:
- 1 avocado, sliced lengthways
- Shop-bought salsa

1 Mix the black beans, sweetcorn, chilli flakes, smoked paprika, spring onions and half the cheese and coriander together, and season with salt and black pepper. Add to your slow cooker, replace the lid for 1 hr 30 mins on high, or 2 hrs 30 mins to 3 hrs on low (if dry during cooking, add a splash of water).
2 Once the filling has cooked, sprinkle a quarter of the cheese over half of one tortilla and top with half of the bean mixture. Top with another handful of cheese and fold the tortilla over.
3 Heat a frying pan over a high heat; , place the quesadilla in the pan and fry for 2 mins or until the cheese has melted slightly. Carefully turn the quesadilla over and cook for 2 mins more. Repeat with remaining tortilla.
4 Cut in half and serve with avocado, salsa and the remaining coriander.

MAIN MEALS

MAIN MEALS

Chilli vegetable hotpot

Instantly warming on a chilly day and delicious with garlic bread

Serves 4 • Ready in 4 hrs 30 mins

- 2tbsp vegetable oil
- 2 onions, chopped
- 2 garlic cloves, crushed
- ½ red chilli, deseeded and chopped
- 450g (15oz) carrots, cut in chunks
- 400g (14oz) tin chopped tomatoes
- 400g (14oz) tin cannellini beans
- ¼ savoy cabbage, shredded
- 350ml (10fl oz) vegetable stock
- Sour cream, chopped basil leaves and lime wedges, to serve

1 Add all the hotpot ingredients to the slow cooker and cook on high for 4 hrs 30 mins.
2 Serve topped with a spoonful of sour cream, a scattering of chopped basil leaves and a lime wedge each.

Fruity chickpea tagine

Packed with punchy flavours, this is vegan-friendly too

Serves 4 • Ready in 4 hrs

- 2tbsp vegetable oil
- 1 onion, chopped
- 1 garlic clove, crushed
- Pinch of saffron threads, crushed
- 1 cinnamon stick
- 1tsp each ground ginger, ground cumin and chilli flakes
- 400g (14oz) tin jackfruit, drained
- 400g (14oz) tin chickpeas, drained
- 10 ready-to-eat dried apricots, halved
- 200g (7oz) tomatoes, roughly chopped
- Juice of 1 lemon
- 1tsp sugar
- 300ml (10fl oz) vegan stock
- 2 preserved lemons, flesh and pith removed
- Handful of coriander, chopped
- Couscous and dairy-free coconut yoghurt, to serve (optional)

1 Heat the oil in a pan, add the onion and garlic, and sauté until softened. Add the spices and sauté for a further 1 min.
2 Add everything from the pan into the slow cooker. Stir in the jackfruit and chickpeas. Add the apricots, tomatoes, lemon juice and sugar. Pour in the stock, cover and cook on high heat for 4 hrs, until tender.
3 Top with lemon and coriander, and serve with couscous and dairy-free yoghurt.

MAIN MEALS

Vegan laksa

Try our deliciously fragrant take on the classic Malaysian noodle broth

Serves 4 • Ready in 3 hrs 15 mins

- 3 medium shallots, sliced roughly
- 3 garlic cloves
- 2 lemongrass stalks, chopped
- 5cm (2in) piece ginger, sliced roughly
- 2 fresh red chillies
- 2tbsp rapeseed oil
- 1tsp ground turmeric
- 1tsp ground coriander
- ½tsp ground cumin
- 1.2l (2.5pt) vegan vegetable stock
- 400ml (14fl oz) full-fat coconut milk
- Juice of 1 lime
- 250g (9oz) firm tofu, cut in cubes
- 1 head broccoli, cut into florets
- 2 baby pak choi, cut in half
- 150g (5oz) sugar snap peas
- 200g (7oz) bean sprouts
- 100g (3.5oz) spinach
- 200g (7oz) flat rice noodles, cooked
- Fresh coriander, chopped
- Chilli flakes, to garnish

1 Make a paste by blitzing together the shallots, garlic, lemongrass, ginger and red chillies. Heat 1tbsp oil on medium in a heavy-based pan, add the paste and fry for 10 mins, stirring occasionally. Add the dry spices and continue to cook for a further 5 mins. Add the ingredients in the pan to the slow cooker.
2 Meanwhile, heat 1 tbsp of oil in a frying pan and fry the tofu until golden. Add to the slow cooker, along with the veg stock, coconut milk, broccoli, pak choi, sugar snaps and bean sprouts. Cook on high for 3 hrs. In the last 10 mins, add the rice noodles and spinach. Season with salt, pepper and the lime juice.
3 Divide the rice noodles between 4 bowls and ladle over the hot broth, veggies and tofu. Garnish with fresh coriander and sprinkle over the chilli flakes.

Cook's Tip
If you want to save time and don't want to fry off the onion, spices and tofu, you can add them directly to the slow cooker.

MAIN MEALS

Butternut squash and sweetcorn korma

This recipe can be tweaked to make it vegan – simply use coconut milk yoghurt

Serves 4 • Ready in 4 hrs 20 mins

- 1tbsp vegetable oil
- 1 red or white onion, peeled and chopped
- 4 cardamom pods, squashed
- 2-3tsp each ground cumin and coriander
- ½-1tsp ground turmeric
- 1 green chilli, deseeded and finely chopped
- 1 garlic clove, peeled and crushed
- 1tbsp grated root ginger
- 1 small butternut squash (around 500g/1lb), peeled, deseeded and cut into chunks
- 1 small cauliflower (around 200g/7oz), broken into big florets
- 1 red pepper, deseeded and cut into big chunks
- 300-600ml (10-20fl oz) hot vegetable stock
- 200g (7oz) mixed frozen soya beans and sweetcorn, thawed
- 150g (5oz) pot natural yoghurt
- 2tbsp ground almonds
- 2-3tbsp flaked almonds, toasted
- A few sprigs of coriander
- Rice or naan bread, to serve

1 Set a slow cooker on low. Heat the oil in a large pan, add the onion with the spices and cook over a low heat for 5-6 mins. Add the chilli, garlic and ginger, stir-fry for 1 min, then tip into the slow cooker pot.
2 Add the squash, cauliflower and pepper, and pour in 300ml (10fl oz) stock. Cook in the slow cooker on low for 4 hrs, until the vegetables are tender.
3 Stir in the beans and sweetcorn, yoghurt and ground almonds. Season and heat through for 10 mins. Scatter with flaked almonds and coriander leaves. Serve with rice or naan bread.

Black bean and roast sweet potato chilli with smoky sour cream

A hearty, meat-free chilli served with fresh, simple accompaniments

Serves 6-8 • Ready in 5-7 hrs

- 500g (1lb) sweet potatoes, cut into 3cm (1.75in) cubes
- 3tbsp olive oil
- 2tsp cumin seeds
- 2tsp coriander seeds
- 1 onion, finely chopped
- 1tsp hot smoked paprika, plus extra to serve
- 2 garlic cloves, finely chopped
- 1 small cinnamon stick
- 3-4tsp chipotle chilli paste
- 2 x 400g (14oz) tins black beans, undrained
- 400g (14oz) tin cherry tomatoes
- 1 bay leaf
- 2tsp cocoa powder
- 250g (9oz) wild rice
- A handful of fresh coriander, chopped, plus extra sprigs to serve
- 2 ripe avocados, halved
- 300ml (10fl oz) sour cream
- Juice of 1 lime, plus 2 limes cut into wedges

1 Heat the oven to 220°C/425°F/Gas 7. Toss the sweet potatoes in 2tbsp of the oil and spread out in a large roasting tin. Roast for 25 mins.
2 Toast the cumin and coriander seeds then crush or grind roughly. Set aside. Heat the remaining oil in a large frying pan, and cook the onion for 8 mins, until softened. Stir in the crushed spices, paprika, garlic and cinnamon stick. Cook for 1 min, stirring, then add 2-3tsp of the chipotle paste, the black beans and their liquid, cherry tomatoes and bay leaf. Transfer the mixture to the slow cooker and add 250ml (9fl oz) water. Cook on low for 4-6 hrs.
3 Check the chilli every now and then, adding extra water if needed. Add the roast sweet potato and cocoa to the slow cooker, turn up the heat and cook for 5 mins more. Check the seasoning, and stir in half the fresh coriander.
4 Cook the wild rice in 900ml (30fl oz) water with a good pinch of salt. Cook, covered for 25-30 mins over a medium heat. Roughly mash the avocados with half the lime juice and salt to taste. Combine the sour cream with the remaining lime juice and seasoning. Marble in the remaining 1tsp chipotle chilli paste.
5 Serve the chilli with the wild rice, avocado, sour cream, lime wedges and coriander sprigs. Scatter with remaining coriander.

MAIN MEALS

MAIN MEALS

MAIN MEALS

Aubergine caponata pasta

A mouth-watering vegetarian dish packed with flavour for an easy supper

Serves 6 • Ready in 3 hrs 30 mins

- 400g (14oz) baby aubergines, quartered
- 2 onions, chopped
- 2 garlic cloves, crushed
- 1 red chilli, thinly sliced
- 2 x 400g (14oz) tins tomatoes
- ½ Knorr Vegetable Stock Pot
- 2tbsp red wine vinegar
- 30g (1oz) black olives, chopped, plus extra to garnish
- 30g (1oz) capers, drained
- 200g (7oz) orzo (rice-shaped pasta)
- 35g (1.5oz) toasted pine nuts
- Handful of chopped parsley and oregano

1 Put the aubergines, onions, garlic, chilli, tomatoes, 1 x 400g (14oz) tin filled with water, the Stock Pot, vinegar, olives and capers into a slow cooker and cook on low for 3 hrs.
2 Add the orzo, stir and cook for 30 mins more. Once tender, serve topped with the remaining olives, the pine nuts and herbs.

> "The caponata sauce can also be served on toasted sourdough"

Ratatouille stew with herbed dumplings

This can be made in one larger dish, if you prefer

Serves 4 • Ready in 6 hrs

- 1 large red onion
- 2 garlic cloves, crushed
- 2 red peppers, cut into chunks
- 2 courgettes, sliced
- 1 aubergine, diced
- 1tbsp olive oil
- 1l (1.75pt) hot vegetable stock
- 400g (14oz) tin cherry tomatoes
- 1tbsp pesto

For the herbed dumplings:
- 125g (4.5oz) self-raising flour
- 60g (2.5oz) vegetable suet
- Handful of basil leaves
- 1tsp thyme leaves

1 Heat the oil in a frying pan. Add the onion and garlic for 5 mins.
2 Put the peppers, courgettes, aubergine, tomatoes, pesto and 300ml (10fl oz) water in the slow cooker and cook for 5 hrs on low.
3 Meanwhile, make the herbed dumplings. Put the flour, vegetable suet, parsley and thyme in a bowl and season generously. Add 100ml (3.5fl oz) cold water and mix everything together. Dust your hands with flour and shape into 4 dumplings.
4 Once the ratatouille is cooked, add the dumplings evenly along the surface and cook for another 1 hr, turning over once.
5 Spoon the ratatouille into 4 ovenproof dishes, put a dumpling into each dish. If you would like to brown them you can place under the grill for 5 mins.

MAIN MEALS

MAIN MEALS

Chicken teriyaki rice bowl

Crunchy, satisfying and healthy – all you need for a quick dinner

Serves 4 • Ready in 2 hr 30 mins, plus chilling

- 6 boneless, skinless chicken thighs, halved
- 3tbsp teriyaki sauce
- 1 onion, halved and sliced
- 1 garlic clove, crushed
- 1 stem lemongrass, sliced
- 2tbsp vegetable oil
- Juice of 1 lime
- 200g (7oz) short-grain rice
- 200g (7oz) Tenderstem broccoli, steamed
- Spring onions, shredded
- Carrots, cut with a julienne peeler and microwaved with 2tbsp water
- 2tbsp rice vinegar
- 1tsp honey
- 1tbsp sesame seeds

1 Season the chicken thighs, piercing them several times with a sharp knife. Put into a non-metallic dish. Drizzle over the teriyaki sauce, onion, garlic, lemongrass, oil and lime juice. Cover and chill for at least 1 hr.
2 Rinse the rice in cold water, drain and put into a pan. Pour over 450ml (16fl oz) cold water and add a pinch of salt. Cover and bring to the boil. Stir. Reduce the heat and simmer for 12-15 mins. Remove from heat and stand, covered, for 10 mins to allow the rice to finish cooking.
3 Heat a wok or frying pan, add the chicken and fry for 5 mins. Add to the slow cooker and cook for 2 hrs on high (you can add to slow cooker without frying, if desired).
4 Mix rice vinegar and honey through the rice. To serve, top with teriyaki chicken, broccoli, spring onions and carrots. Sprinkle over sesame seeds.

MAIN MEALS

Chicken giouvetsi (orzo chicken pasta)

A centuries-old Greek classic, giouvetsi is both perfectly light and incredibly comforting at the same time. Feel free to substitute the chicken for lamb or your favourite meat

Serves 4 • Ready in 1 hr 50 mins

- 4 chicken thighs
- 2tbsp Greek olive oil
- 3 shallots, finely sliced
- 2 celery sticks, finely diced
- 3 garlic cloves, crushed
- 150ml (5fl oz) white wine
- 400g (14oz) tin chopped tomatoes
- 1 cinnamon stick
- 200ml (7fl oz) water
- 1tsp sugar
- 250g (9oz) orzo pasta
- 100g (3.5oz) olives
- 1 small bunch of parsley, finely chopped
- 4tbsp grated Pecorino Romano, to serve

1 Heat the slow cooker for 10 mins.
2 In a frying pan, fry the shallots and celery together until light brown and then add the garlic and cook it off.
3 Add the cooked shallots, celery and garlic to the slow cooker.
4 Add the chicken thighs, wine, chopped tomatoes, olives, cinnamon stick, salt and pepper
5 Cook on high for 1 hr 10 mins and then add the orzo and 200ml (7fl oz) of water. Cook for a further 30 mins.
6 Once cooked, add pecorino romano and parsley, to serve.

"This slow-cooked Greek dish can also be made with beef or lamb and hilopites, a small square-shaped pasta"

Chicken and chorizo paella

Impressive enough to serve to guests, but easy enough to whip up for an everyday meal

Serves 6 • Ready in 2 hrs, plus prep

- 3tbsp olive oil
- 4 chicken breasts, cut into chunks
- 1tbsp chicken seasoning
- 2 red onions, peeled and roughly chopped
- 2 garlic cloves, puréed
- 225g (8oz) chorizo, sliced
- Juice of 1 lemon
- 2 red peppers, deseeded and cut in chunks
- 2 x 175g (6oz) packets of risotto rice (we used Gallo Risotto Pronto Saffron)
- 1tsp sun-dried tomato paste
- 3tbsp chives, chopped

1 Switch the slow cooker on high and add 3tbsp of olive oil.
2 Season the chicken with the chicken seasoning and pepper.
3 Add the puréed garlic to the oil in the slow cooker. Then add the chopped onion, chorizo and chicken.
4 Add the lemon juice, peppers, risotto rice, 900ml (30fl oz) water and tomato paste. Stir, then cover and cook for 2 hrs on high, until the rice is tender and the water is absorbed.
5 Serve up the paella and sprinkle with chives.

MAIN MEALS

Cook's Tip
Save leftovers for a delicious cold lunch the following day.

MAIN MEALS

Roast chicken with lemon and herbs

Add spring flavours to a good-quality chicken with a seasonal salad

Serves 6 • Ready in 3 hrs

- 1 medium free-range chicken, about 1.5kg/3lb
- Small bunch each of lemon thyme and rosemary
- 4 preserved lemons, halved
- A little oil
- 4tsp dried chervil

For the salad:
- 150g (5oz) runner beans
- 250g (9oz) broad beans
- 150g (5oz) green beans
- 3tbsp mustard vinaigrette

1 Put the thyme and rosemary into the cavity of the chicken with the lemons. Rub the oil into the skin.
2 Place the chicken into the slow cooker (it may need to go in at an angle depending on the size and shape of your slow cooker).
3 Cook for 3 hrs on high (turning the chicken half way through), or until cooked through and the juices of the thickest part of the thigh run clear. Leave to rest and sprinkle over the dried chervil. Reheat the juices to serve.
2 Blanch the beans then refresh under cold running water. Mix them with the vinaigrette, to serve with some new potatoes on the side. Carve the chicken or cut into joints.

Super easy chicken curry

When only a curry will do, you can get this on the table fast!

Serves 4 • Ready in 4 hrs

- 1tbsp groundnut oil
- 1 red onion, sliced
- 500g (1lb) chicken fillets
- 4-6tbsp tikka masala paste
- 200g (7oz) tin of chopped tomatoes
- Handful of fresh spinach leaves
- Handful of fresh coriander leaves
- Mini naan breads, to serve

1 Heat the groundnut oil in a wok or large frying pan. Add the sliced red onion and fry gently for 5 mins.
2 Add the chicken fillets to the pan and cook for 10 mins, turning as needed, until golden. Add to the slow cooker.
3 Add the tikka masala paste (check the instructions on the jar for exact amounts), 100ml (3.5fl oz) water and the tin of chopped tomatoes. Cook on high for 4 hrs.
5 Finally, add the fresh spinach leaves and stir in to wilt. Garnish the curry with fresh coriander leaves and serve immediately with the mini naans.

"Make your own tikka masala paste using garlic, ginger coriander, chilli cumin, tomato paste and oil"

MAIN MEALS

MAIN MEALS

Creamy cider chicken casserole

This easy, classic dish is tasty comfort food at its best

Serves 4 • Ready in 4 hrs 20 mins

- 2 chicken breasts, halved
- 4 chicken drumsticks, skin removed
- 25g (1oz) butter
- 4 rashers streaky bacon, chopped
- 8 shallots, peeled
- 3 sticks celery, chopped
- 2 eating apples, cut into wedges
- 300ml (10fl oz) cider or apple juice
- 500ml (17fl oz) chicken stock
- 1tbsp thickening granules
- 100ml (3.5fl oz) crème fraîche
- 2tbsp Dijon mustard
- 2tbsp tarragon

1 Season the chicken. Melt the butter in a large frying pan and fry the chicken for 10 mins, turning to brown all over.
2 Add the bacon, shallots, celery and apples. Cook for a few mins. Remove apples and add all the ingredients, plus the cider and stock to the slow cooker. Cook for 4 hrs on high, until the chicken is tender.
3 When cooked, ladle out some of the liquid and add to a pan with the thickening granules, apple, crème fraîche, mustard and tarragon. Stir on a low heat until the sauce thickens. Then add into the casserole and stir. Serve with a side of mashed potato.

Summer slow cooker cheesy chicken bake

Your slow cooker can free up time for you to spend outdoors!

Serves 5 • Ready in 4 hrs

- 8 skinless, boneless chicken thighs
- 2tbsp seasoned flour
- 1 onion, sliced
- 250g (9oz) button mushrooms
- 3 garlic cloves, crushed
- 2tsp fresh thyme leaves
- 200ml (7fl oz) hot chicken stock
- 2 x 30g (1oz) bags unsalted crisps
- 100g (3.5oz) cheese, grated

1 In a large plastic food bag, shake the chicken with the seasoned flour until well coated. Put in the bottom of the slow cooker.
2 Add the onion slices, mushrooms, garlic and thyme to the pot. Pour over hot stock, cover and set the slow cooker to high. Cook for 3-4 hrs.
3 Serve, giving each guest cheese and crispy topping to sprinkle on the top.

"This family dish is also only 388 calories per serving if you're looking for a lighter option"

MAIN MEALS

Cook's Tip
Using crisps here might sound odd, but they add seasoning and a good crunch. Who doesn't love crisps?

MAIN MEALS

Moroccan tagine

A fabulous dish using either chicken or lamb. The slow cooker really helps make this one soft and juicy

Serves 4 • Ready in 6 hrs 10 mins, plus soaking

- 125g (4.5oz) dried chickpeas
- 2tbsp groundnut oil
- 500g (1lb) chicken thighs
- 1 large onion, chopped
- 2tsp ground ginger
- 2tsp ground cinnamon
- 2tsp turmeric
- 500g (1lb) pumpkin, peeled and cubed
- 2 celery stalks, chopped
- Pinch of saffron threads
- 2 x 400g (14oz) tins tomatoes
- 1l (1.75pt) chicken stock
- 60g (3.5oz) dried red lentils
- 2tbsp coriander leaves
- 8 green olives

To serve:
- Giant couscous
- Pomegranate seeds

1 Soak the chickpeas in cold water for several hrs. Heat the oil in a large frying pan, add the chicken, and brown for 5 mins.
2 Add the onion, ginger, cinnamon and turmeric, and cook for a few mins to soften and cook the spices.
3 Add all the ingredients in the pan, together with the pumpkin, celery, saffron, tomatoes, stock, drained soaked chickpeas and red lentils into the slow cooker. Cover and cook for 6 hrs on low.
4 Allow to cool before freezing, then defrost completely and reheat to serve. To serve, sprinkle with coriander leaves and olives, and serve with giant couscous and pomegranate seeds.

MAIN MEALS

Cook's Tip
Prepare the tagine and freeze. Defrost and reheat to serve with the couscous.

MAIN MEALS

Cook's Tip
Bake in oven with corn chips, jalapeño peppers, sweetcorn and cheese. Serve with sour cream and coriander.

MAIN MEALS

Chipotle pulled chicken with slaw

Perfect for an easy Friday night in, this spicy number makes enough for two meals – leftovers will taste even better the next day!

Serves 8-12 • Ready in 3-5 hrs

- 1.2kg (2.5lb) skinless chicken thighs
- 1 x 400g (14oz) tin chopped tomatoes
- 2 red onions, finely chopped
- 4 garlic cloves, crushed
- 2-3tbsp chipotle paste (depending how spicy you like it)
- Slaw, tortillas and chopped coriander, to serve (optional)

1 Combine all the ingredients in a slow cooker and season to taste. Cook on low for 5 hrs or on high for 3 hrs. Shred the meat with two forks and mix through the sauce.
2 Serve half the chicken with a crunchy slaw, warm tortillas and chopped coriander. Chill the remaining stew in an airtight container in a refrigerator for 1-2 days or freeze for up to 3 months.

"Like a thicker sauce? Just use thickening granules. You can also use orange or lemon zest rather than pickled lemon, if you prefer"

North African Chicken

North African cooking is warm and fragrant with spice. This recipe uses the classic harissa paste to flavour meaty chicken thighs

Serves 4-6 • Ready in 3 hrs, plus marinating

- 4-6tsp harissa paste
- 8 chicken thighs, trimmed of excess fat and excess skin
- 1tbsp olive oil
- 2 onions, peeled and thickly sliced
- 2-3 garlic cloves, peeled and sliced
- 2 sweet potatoes or 4 medium potatoes, or a mixture of the two, peeled and cut into big chunks
- 2 pickled lemons, rinsed and sliced (scoop out the flesh and slice skin)
- 600ml (1pt) hot chicken stock
- 150ml (5fl oz) tub Greek yoghurt
- Handful of chopped coriander
- Couscous, pittas or rice, to serve

1 If you have time, rub half the harissa paste into the chicken thighs and marinate them for 1-4 hrs or overnight.
2 Preheat your slow-cooker pot for 10 mins.
3 Warm the oil in a large frying pan, add the chicken and fry on each side until browned. Set aside. Pour off almost all the fat in the pan, then add the onion and garlic to the pan.
4 Add the rest of the harissa paste and cook for 1 min. Add the potato chunks, pickled lemon and stock. Bring to the boil. Pour into the pot, then put the chicken thighs in and cook for 3 hrs on high.
5 Season, then serve topped with a dollop of yoghurt and sprinkle of coriander. Serve with couscous, pitta bread or red rice.

MAIN MEALS

Chinese five-spice chicken with sweetcorn

This not only makes an easy and delicious dinner, but this fakeaway is under 500 calories

Serves 4 • Ready in 5 hrs

- 1 onion, peeled and thinly sliced
- 2 garlic cloves, sliced
- 1tbsp Chinese five-spice powder
- ½tbsp Sichuan peppercorns
- 60ml (2.5fl oz) soy sauce
- 90ml (3.5fl oz) honey
- 1.5kg (3lb) chicken thighs, bone in (6-8 thighs, depending on size)
- Coriander, to garnish (optional)

For the sweetcorn
- 4 corn on the cobs
- 20g (0.75oz) butter
- Splash soy sauce
- Pinch dried chilli flakes

1 In a large dish, mix the onion, garlic, five-spice powder, peppercorns, soy sauce and honey until smooth. Add the chicken thighs and coat well in the sauce. Cover with clingfilm and leave in the fridge for at least 1 hr or up to two days.
2 Add the chicken mixture to a slow cooker and cook on high for 4 hrs. Sprinkle with coriander to serve.
3 For the sweetcorn, stand the cobs upright, then run a knife down the cob to cut off the kernels. Stir-fry in butter, soy sauce and a pinch of dried chilli flakes for 2-3 mins. Spoon into a bowl and serve on the side.

Chicken pilaf -style rice

This flavoursome one-pot dinner makes light work of meal prep

Serves 4-6 • Ready in 2 hrs 30 mins

- 250g (9oz) basmati rice
- 1 large onion, thinly sliced
- 2tbsp curry paste (we used Patak's madras paste)
- 4-6 chicken thighs, cut into chunks
- 400ml (14oz) tin light coconut milk
- 200ml (7fl oz) water or stock
- 2tbsp oil
- 100ml (3.5fl oz) water or stock
- 25g (1oz) dried cranberries (optional)
- Coriander, to garnish (optional)

1 Rinse the rice then leave to soak while you prepare the rest.
2 In a frying pan, fry the onion in 2tbsp oil until caramelised. Set some aside for the garnish,
3 Add the curry paste to the onion in the frying pan and cook it off for at least 2 mins.
4 Add the chicken thighs and cook for 2 mins until light brown.
5 Put the onions, curry paste and chicken in the slow cooker and add 200ml (7fl oz) of water, the coconut milk and drained rice. Cook on low for 2 hrs 30 mins.
5 Top with the reserved caramelised onion, cranberries and freshly chopped coriander, if liked.

"Top with chopped or toasted almonds if you want to add a bit of crunch"

MAIN MEALS

MAIN MEALS

Lighter chicken Milanese

Our twist includes a flavoursome crunchy crumb and is served with a rich tomatoey pasta. Great when time is short midweek

Serves 2 • Ready in 2 hrs 30 mins

- 2½tsp olive oil, plus extra for brushing
- 2 garlic cloves, puréed
- 400g (14oz) tin cherry tomatoes
- 1tbsp balsamic vinegar
- ½tsp smoked paprika
- 120g (4oz) bucatini spaghetti or other long pasta shape
- 2tbsp capers, drained
- 2tbsp breadcrumbs
- 2tbsp finely grated Parmesan
- ½tsp dried oregano
- 2 free-range skinless chicken breasts, seasoned and sliced
- 1tbsp fresh oregano or basil

1 Switch the slow cooker on to high. Add 2tbsp olive oil, the sliced chicken breasts and stir.
2 Add the cherry tomatoes, balsamic vinegar, paprika and seasoning. Stir and cook for 2 hrs 30 mins on low.
3 Heat 1tsp oil in a non-stick frying pan. Fry the capers for 3 mins, stir in the breadcrumbs and toast until golden. Transfer to a bowl and mix in the Parmesan, oregano and a grind of black pepper.
4 Cook and drain the pasta, then toss with the tomato sauce until well coated.
5 Divide between 2 plates. Top the chicken with the toasted breadcrumb mixture and fresh oregano or basil, if liked.

Cook's Tip
This recipe is easy to double to serve more people.

MAIN MEALS

Lemongrass and ginger chicken

Warming lemongrass, ginger and garlic are all good for helping to fight winter coughs and colds

Serves 4 • Prep 10 mins, plus marinating • Cook 4-6 hrs (low), plus 5-10 mins frying

For the marinade:
- 2tbsp fish sauce
- 1tbsp caster sugar
- 3 sticks lemongrass, roughly chopped
- 3 garlic cloves, peeled
- 6cm (2.5in) piece ginger, peeled and roughly chopped
- 8 large chicken thighs
- 1-2tbsp groundnut oil
- Juice of 1 lime, plus wedges to serve
- 2tbsp chopped fresh coriander, plus extra leaves to serve
- Jasmine rice, to serve

1 Blitz all the ingredients for the marinade in a blender or food processor. Add to a large bowl along with the chicken thighs and stir to coat. Cover and chill in the fridge for at least 30 mins, or overnight.
2 Once marinated, heat the oil in a large pan over a medium-high heat. Remove the chicken from the marinade, add to the pan and brown well on all sides. Once browned, add the marinade to the pan and continue to fry for 1 min until fragrant.
3 Transfer the chicken and marinade mix to the bowl of your slow cooker. If the sauce doesn't cover the bottom of the bowl, add a little water 1tbsp at a time until it does (add extra water if you prefer a thinner sauce). Stir well, then cook on low for 4-6 hrs, until the chicken is cooked through and deliciously tender.
4 Once cooked, stir in the lime juice and chopped coriander, taste and season. Serve with jasmine rice, lime wedges and extra coriander.

The Ultimate Slow Cooker Cookbook

MAIN MEALS

MAIN MEALS

Coq au champagne

A fabulous celebratory twist on the classic chicken dish – although any sparkling wine will work if you prefer to save the posh stuff for drinking!

Serves 4 • Ready in 3-7 hrs

- 2tbsp olive oil
- 4 chicken breasts, skin on
- 2 sticks celery, finely chopped
- 300g (10.5oz) pearl shallots, peeled
- 2 carrots, roughly chopped
- 350g (12oz) small chestnut mushrooms or larger ones, quartered
- 2 sprigs thyme
- 350ml (12oz) champagne
- 125ml (4.5fl oz) chicken stock
- Few sprigs tarragon leaves, chopped
- 3tbsp crème fraîche
- Lemon wedges, to serve

1 Heat half the oil in a large, lidded frying pan and fry the chicken skin side down. Season the top of the chicken and leave it to cook until the skin is crisp and golden. Turn it over, season the skin and cook for a further 5 mins. Remove the chicken from the pan and place in your slow cooker, skin facing up.
2 Add the remaining oil to the pan along with the celery, shallots and carrots. Cook on a low heat for 5 mins. Transfer to the slow cooker.
3 Pour in the champagne to deglaze your frying pan, using a wooden spoon to scrape off any residue. Transfer the champagne and scrapings to the slow cooker.
4 Add the mushrooms, thyme and chicken stock, cover and cook for 3-4 hrs on high, or 6-7 hrs on low.
5 Half an hour before serving, remove the lid to allow the sauce to thicken up, or transfer to a saucepan and reduce on a low heat. Stir in the crème fraîche and top with tarragon. Serve with potatoes or rice.
6 To freeze and reheat: cool completely, place in a container and freeze for up to 3 months. To serve, defrost, reheat and stir through the tarragon and crème fraîche.

Cook's Tip
This recipe also works really well with chicken legs or thighs.

MAIN MEALS

Bombay braised chicken

A hearty all-in-one meal that takes care of itself

Serves 4 • Ready in 2 hrs 30 mins, plus marinating

- 2tbsp sunflower oil
- 3cm (1.75in) piece ginger, peeled
- 3 garlic cloves, peeled
- 1 red chilli
- 1tsp each ground cumin, ground coriander and garam masala
- ½tsp ground turmeric
- 1tsp fennel seeds
- 4 chicken leg portions
- 300ml (10.5fl oz) chicken stock
- 400g (14oz) new potatoes, halved if large
- 250g (9oz) cauliflower, cut into florets
- 200g (7oz) green beans
- A few fresh coriander leaves

1 To make the spice paste, whizz together 1tbsp oil, the ginger, garlic and chilli until smooth. Add the spices and fennel seeds, and stir to mix. Rub the paste over the chicken and season (skin can be removed). Marinate in the fridge for at least 2 hrs.
2 Add the remaining ingredients to the slow cooker, except for the cauliflower and green beans. Make sure the chicken is submerged in the marinade. Cook for 1.5 hrs on high.
3 Add the cauliflower and cook for 30 mins, adding the green beans in for the last 10 mins. Scatter with coriander to serve.

"Make it an Indian feast and serve with poppadoms and chutney"

Spicy prawn and chicken jambalaya

Originating from Louisiana, this Deep South dish has Spanish influences and a moreish flavour

Serves 6 • Ready in 2 hr 30 mins

- 2tbsp olive oil
- 6 chicken thighs, chopped
- 125g (5oz) smoked sausage or chorizo, sliced
- 1 red onion, diced
- 1 red pepper, diced
- 1 green pepper, diced
- 2 sticks celery, diced
- 3 garlic cloves, crushed
- 1 bay leaf
- 1 large sprig thyme
- 1½tbsp Cajun seasoning
- 300g (10oz) long grain rice
- 400g (13.5oz) tin plum tomatoes
- 500ml (18fl oz) chicken stock
- 180g (6oz) raw prawns
- Tabasco, to taste

1 In a large frying pan, heat the oil over a medium heat and sauté the chicken thighs and sausage until just brown.
2 Add along with the onion, pepper, celery and garlic to the slow cooker. Add the bay leaf, thyme, Cajun seasoning, plum tomatoes and chicken stock. Cook on high for 2.5 hrs, stirring occasionally.
3 Add the prawns and Tabasco to taste 15 mins before the end and cook until the prawns are pink.
4 Serve with a green salad or crusty bread on the side.

MAIN MEALS

Cook's Tip
For an authentic taste, look for Andouille sausages.

The Ultimate Slow Cooker Cookbook **61**

MAIN MEALS

Turkey, butternut squash and coconut curry

A light, fresh curry that will perk up the tastebuds after Christmas. Equally good with leftover chicken or cooked, peeled prawns

Serves 4 • Ready in 2 hrs

- 450g (1lb) butternut squash, peeled, deseeded and cut into 2cm (0.75in) cubes
- 2tbsp sunflower oil
- 1 onion, halved and sliced
- 1tbsp Thai red curry paste
- 400ml (14fl oz) tin coconut milk
- 250ml (9fl oz) chicken stock
- 2tbsp fish sauce
- 1tsp sugar
- 4 kaffir lime leaves
- 100g (3.5oz) fine green beans, trimmed and halved
- 350g (12oz) cooked turkey, cut into large strips
- Juice of 1 lime
- 2tbsp coriander chopped, plus some for garnish
- 1 red chilli, deseeded and thinly sliced

1 Heat the oil in a large frying pan and sweat the onion for 5 mins until soft.

2 Place the butternut squash, Thai red curry paste, coconut milk, chicken stock, fish sauce, sugar and kaffir leaves in the slow cooker. Cook for 2 hrs on high.

3 Add the green beans and turkey 20 mins before the end of the 2 hrs. Stir in the lime juice and coriander. Have a taste – you may need a little more lime juice.

4 To serve, scatter over the chilli and remaining coriander leaves. Serve with jasmine rice.

MAIN MEALS

Chicken korma

Ditch the takeaway for a lovely homemade curry that tastes great and isn't full of additives

Serves 4 • Ready in 3-7 hrs

- 2 small onions, chopped
- 3 garlic cloves, grated
- 1tbsp rapeseed oil
- 4 skinless chicken breasts
- 6 cloves
- 6 cardamom pods
- 1 small cinnamon stick
- ½tsp turmeric
- ½tsp gluten free red chilli powder
- 100ml (3.5fl oz) chicken stock
- 200ml (7fl oz) coconut milk
- 250g (9oz) brown rice
- 45g (1.5oz) desiccated coconut
- 2tbsp natural yoghurt
- Large handful of coriander leaves, finely chopped
- 1 lime, cut into wedges

1 Blend the onions and garlic in a food processor until smooth. Set aside.
2 Place chicken breasts at the bottom of your slow cooker. Cover with the onion and garlic paste, cloves, cardamom, cinnamon stick, turmeric, chilli powder and the chicken stock. Cook for 6-7 hrs on low, or 3-4 hrs on high.
3 Half an hr before serving, remove the lid and either shred the chicken with a fork, or chop into large chunks. Stir in the coconut milk and leave the lid off to allow the sauce to thicken up.
4 Meanwhile, cook the rice according to pack instructions.
5 Heat a pan to hot, add the desiccated coconut and toast for 1-2 mins until golden. Just before serving, stir toasted coconut through the curry, along with the yoghurt. Serve with the rice and chopped coriander. Garnish with lime wedges.

Cook's Tip
Serve with cauliflower rice if you're cutting down on carbs and calories.

MAIN MEALS

Chicken meatballs in red veg sauce with fettuccine

Using chicken makes these lighter than traditional beef meatballs – so you can eat more!

Serves 4 • Ready in 2 hrs 30 mins

- 500g (1lb) chicken mince (we used breast and thigh)
- 3 spring onions, roughly chopped
- 25g (1oz) Parmesan, grated, plus extra to garnish
- 30g (1.5oz) basil, reserving a few leaves for garnish
- 1tbsp olive oil
- 2 roasted red peppers, roughly chopped
- 3tbsp sundried tomato purée
- 600ml (21fl oz) cherry tomato pasta sauce
- 400g (14oz) dried fettuccine

1 Tip the chicken mince into a food processor along with the spring onions, grated Parmesan and basil (keeping the reserved leaves to one side). Whizz until combined, then tip into a large bowl. Season to taste.
2 Divide the chicken mixture into 4, then roll each quarter into 5 equal-size meatballs. Heat the olive oil in a large frying pan and brown the meatballs over a high heat for 2 mins.
3 Tip the roasted red peppers into a blender with the sundried tomato purée and whizz until smooth. Add the tomato sauce and whizz again.
4 Add the sauce to the slow cooker and then add the meatballs in so they are half covered with sauce. Cook for 2 hrs on high.
5 Meanwhile, cook the fettuccine in boiling salted water for 10-12 minutes until al dente. Divide the pasta between 4 bowls and top with the meatballs and sauce. Sprinkle with the remaining Parmesan and garnish with the reserved basil leaves.

Chicken Thai red curry

For perfect, stress-free cooking, buy a super-moist rotisserie chicken to save on cooking time

Serves 4 • Ready in 3 hrs 30 mins

- 1tbsp oil
- 6tbsp red Thai curry paste
- 2 medium potatoes, peeled and diced into 1cm (0.5in) cubes
- 1 red pepper, cut into 1cm (0.5in) strips
- 1 red onion, cut into 1cm (0.5in) strips
- 2cm (1in) piece of fresh ginger, peeled and puréed
- 400ml (14fl oz) coconut cream
- 200ml (7fl oz) water
- 1tbsp Thai fish sauce
- 1tbsp palm sugar or light brown sugar
- 1 rotisserie chicken, meat removed

To serve:
- 200g (7oz) canned water chestnuts, drained
- 100g (3.5oz) spinach
- Thai basil, to serve

1 Switch the slow cooker on high and add the oil.
2 Add the red onion, red Thai curry paste, ginger, Thai fish sauce, sugar, red pepper, potatoes, water and coconut cream to the slow cooker. Give it all a good stir and cook on high for 3 hrs 30 mins.
3 Add the chicken for the last 30 mins of cooking time and in the last 5 mins add the water chestnuts and spinach.
4 Stir through the Thai basil and serve with basmati rice.

MAIN MEALS

MAIN MEALS

Chicken cacciatore

Marinated in red wine for a rich flavour and signature colour too

Serves 4-6 • Ready in 3 hr 10 mins, plus marinating

- 6 skin-on, bone-in free-range chicken thighs
- 300ml (10fl oz) red wine
- ½ bunch each thyme, oregano and rosemary
- 8 bay leaves
- 8 garlic cloves, finely sliced
- 2tbsp flour
- 2tbsp olive oil
- 1 large onion, finely sliced
- 6 anchovy fillets
- 2 x 400g (14oz) tins plum tomatoes
- 200g (7oz) fresh tomatoes, diced
- 2tbsp sun-dried tomato paste
- 200g (7oz) mixed olives

1 Cover the chicken in the red wine and herbs, and add 1 sliced garlic clove. Leave to marinate for at least 2 hrs, or overnight if possible.
2 Drain the chicken from the marinating liquid (reserving it for cooking). Dust the chicken in flour and season well. Add the oil to a large pan and fry the chicken, skin side down, for 5 mins until golden. Remove from the pan.
3 Add chicken to the slow cooker (you can also skip step 2, remove the skin from the chicken and add straight to the slow cooker) along with the onion, anchovies and remaining garlic. Stir through all the tomatoes, the tomato paste, reserved marinade and olives. Cook for 3 hrs, until the meat is cooked through.
4 Serve with green beans.

Cook's Tip
These recipes make the perfect get-ahead food, as the flavour of a good stew just gets better if left overnight.

MAIN MEALS

MAIN MEALS

Cook's Tip
Replace the turkey with prawns or extra veg, depending on what you have to hand.

MAIN MEALS

Cook's Tip
Finish the recipe, allow the stew to cool and freeze until needed.

Thai-style turkey and noodle soup

Craving something healthy? This spicy soup is just the ticket!

Serves 4 • Ready in 1 hr 10 mins

- 125g (4.5oz) Thai rice noodles
- 2tbsp Thai red curry paste
- 2 x 400ml (14fl oz) tins coconut milk
- 200g (7oz) cooked leftover turkey, broken into pieces
- 1 bunch spring onions, sliced
- 1 red pepper, deseeded and sliced
- Finely grated zest and juice of 1 lime
- Dash of fish sauce
- Pinch of sugar
- Fresh coriander, for garnish

1 Cook the pepper, Thai red curry paste, and coconut milk in the slow cooker for 1 hr on high.
2 Add the turkey, noodles, spring onions, lime zest, fish sauce and sugar and cook for another 10 mins on low (about 40 mins if using egg noodles).
3 Garnish with coriander to serve.

"This is a great way to use up turkey left over from a roast and you can make it with egg noodles too"

Chicken and vegetable stew

Perfect for a spring evening meal

Serves 4 • Ready in 4-8 hrs

- 2tbsp oil
- 2 onions, finely chopped
- 4 chicken breasts on the bone, skin removed
- 2 Knorr Chicken Stock Pot
- 3tsp Dijon mustard
- 3 large potatoes, quartered
- 3 carrots, quartered lengthways
- 2 leeks, sliced
- 2tbsp chopped chives (optional)
- 4tbsp crème fraîche
- 2tsp thickening granules

1 Heat the oil in a frying pan, add the onions and cook for a few mins to soften.
2 Season the chicken generously, add to the pan and press down. Cook for 10 mins, turning once to brown.
3 Add to the slow cooker, along with 300ml (10fl oz) boiling water, Stock Pots, mustard, potatoes, carrots, leeks and chives, if using. Cover and cook for 4 hrs on high or 8 hrs on low.
5 Stir in the thickening granules until combined. Stir in the crème fraîche and serve.

The Ultimate Slow Cooker Cookbook

MAIN MEALS

Cook's Tip
You can also serve this with polenta or creamy mashed potato.

Italian lamb shank stew

Everyone will think this rich casserole is drenched in wine, but it's actually alcohol free!

Serves 4 • Ready in 8 hrs

- 30g (1.5oz) dried porcini dried mushrooms
- 4 small lamb shanks
- 1tbsp poultry seasoning (we used Bart)
- 2tbsp olive oil
- 1 large onion, chopped
- 2 celery sticks, chopped
- 150ml (5fl oz) balsamic vinegar
- 2 x 400g (14oz) tins chopped tomatoes
- 1tbsp sundried tomato paste
- 500g (1lb) baby Chantenay carrots
- 2 x 400g (14oz) tins of cannellini beans, drained and rinsed
- Crusty bread, to serve

1 Put the dried mushrooms in a bowl and cover with 100ml (3.5fl oz) of boiling water to soften.
2 Sprinkle the lamb shanks with poultry seasoning, salt and ground black pepper. Heat the oil in a large flameproof frying pan, add the lamb and brown for 10 mins, turning as needed.
3 Add to the slow cooker along with the onion and celery. Then tip in the dried mushrooms and soaking liquid.
4 Pour in the vinegar, tomatoes, tomato paste and carrots. Cook for 8 hrs on low until the meat and vegetables are tender. Stir in the cannellini beans and heat through. Serve with crusty bread.

MAIN MEALS

Harissa lamb and feta pasta shells

This one-tray sauce packs lots of flavour with not many ingredients

Serves 4-6 • Prep 20 mins • Cook 1 hr 25 mins

- 500g (1lb) lamb mince
- Small red onion, finely sliced
- Olive oil, for drizzling
- 300g (10.5oz) pasta shells
- 2tbsp rose harissa
- Zest and juice 1 lemon
- 200g (7oz) block feta
- 500ml (17fl oz) chicken stock
- 2tbsp toasted pine nuts
- Handful freshly chopped dill
- Yoghurt, to serve

1 Heat the oil in a frying pan and brown the red onion and lamb mince for 15 mins.
2 Remove excess oil from the pan with paper towel and tip it all into the slow cooker.
3 Mix the harissa with the lemon zest and juice. Drizzle over the meat and onion, and mix. Add the chicken stock and pasta and cook on high for 1 hr 10 mins, stirring half way.
4 Once cooked, break up the feta and add it in.
5 Plate up and scatter with the toasted pine nuts, dill and some yoghurt.

"Mint also works well with this dish if you don't have any dill"

Cook's Tip
This works with turkey mince, or make it veggie with a plant-based version.

The Ultimate Slow Cooker Cookbook 71

MAIN MEALS

Persian-style lamb stew

Whip up a big batch of this warming lamb stew and have dinners sorted for days. It only gets better!

Serves 8 • Ready in 4-6 hrs

- 1.5kg (3lb) cubed lamb shoulder, excess fat trimmed
- 2tbsp olive oil
- 3 onions, finely chopped
- 4 garlic cloves, bashed
- 5cm (2in) piece ginger, grated
- 1tsp ground cumin
- 1tsp ground coriander
- ½tsp ground cloves
- Zest 2 lemons or 1 orange
- 60ml (2.5fl oz) pomegranate molasses (or balsamic vinegar)
- 200ml (7fl oz) low-sodium lamb or beef stock
- Couscous, yoghurt and a fresh cucumber and herb salad, to serve (optional)

1 Combine the lamb stew ingredients in a slow cooker and season. Cook on low for 6 hrs or high for 4 hrs.
2 Serve half the lamb stew with couscous, yoghurt and a fresh, crunchy cucumber and herb salad. Chill the remaining stew in an airtight container for 2-3 days or freeze for up to 3 months.

Cook's Tip
For a lighter option or lunch serve the stew over quinoa.

MAIN MEALS

Spicy lamb meatballs in sherry sauce

Sweet and savoury flavours combine to give a mouthwatering tapas-style treat

Serves 6 • Ready in 6 hrs

For the meatballs:
- 1tsp cumin seeds
- 1tsp coriander seeds
- Good pinch of dried chilli flakes
- 1-2 garlic cloves, peeled and crushed
- 30g (1oz) breadcrumbs
- 2tbsp chopped fresh parsley
- 450g (1lb) lean lamb mince
- 72g (2.5oz) pack thinly sliced Serrano ham, finely chopped
- 2tbsp olive oil

For the sauce:
- 1 onion, chopped
- 4 garlic cloves, crushed
- Good pinch dried chilli flakes
- 2tbsp olive oil
- 2 x 400g (14oz) tins chopped tomatoes
- 275ml (9fl oz) fino sherry
- 300ml (10fl oz) chicken or vegetable stock
- 1 bay leaf
- Chopped parsley and crusty wholemeal bread, to serve

1 For the meatballs, grind the cumin, coriander seeds and chilli flakes together, then tip into a large bowl and add the garlic, breadcrumbs, parsley, mince and ham. Season well and mix to combine. Shape the mixture into 30 small balls.

2 Heat the oil in a large frying pan, add the meatballs and cook for 4-5 mins, until browned. Drain on kitchen paper and leave to one side.

3 For the sauce, fry the onion, garlic and chilli flakes in the oil for 8-10 mins, until softened.

4 Add the onion mixture, meatballs, tomatoes, sherry, stock and bay leaf to the slow cooker and cook on low for 6 hrs. Season to taste.

5 Sprinkle with chopped parsley and serve with crusty bread.

MAIN MEALS

MAIN MEALS

Slow roasted Provençale lamb

Tender, delicious, slow-cooked meat – best with French beans and roast potatoes

Serves 6 • Ready in 5 hrs 10 mins

- 1.25kg (3lb) half a leg or shoulder of lamb
- 4 garlic cloves, sliced a few rosemary stalks
- 3tbsp balsamic vinegar
- 2tsp all-purpose seasoning
- 2 onions, sliced
- 2 large heads of fennel, sliced
- 4tbsp olive oil
- 400g (14oz) midi plum tomatoes
- 100g (3.5oz) Kalamata olives
- A few parsley leaves

1 Slash the lamb in several places and push in 2 of the garlic cloves and rosemary leaves
2 Warm the slow cooker up for 10 mins. Add the onions, fennel, plum tomatoes, olives, and 4tbsp water. Then add the lamb.
3 Mix together 4tbsp of olive oil and the 3tbsp of balsamic vinegar. Drizzle over the meat. Season and sprinkle over all-purpose seasoning. Cook for 1 hr on high and then a further 4 hrs on low.
4 Garnish the cooked lamb with the parsley to serve.

MAIN MEALS

Spring lamb stew

The simplest of flavours using the bounty of spring

Serves 4 • Ready in 3 hrs 10 mins

- 1tbsp vegetable oil
- 500g (1lb) lean leg of lamb, cut into large chunks
- 4-6 shallots, peeled and halved if large
- 2-4 small turnips, peeled and halved
- 500g (1lb) new potatoes, whole or halved
- 200g (7oz) Chantenay carrots
- 2 leeks, trimmed and cut into thick slices
- 600ml (20fl oz) hot lamb or chicken stock
- About 1tbsp thickening granules
- 200g (7oz) frozen peas
- Handful of freshly chopped mint and whole mint leaves, to garnish

1 Heat the oil in a large pan, then brown the meat over a high heat for a few mins on each side. Add the meat, along with the shallots, turnips, potatoes, carrots and leeks to the slow cooker.
2 Pour the stock over the meat and vegetables, cover and cook for 2 hrs 45 mins.
3 Ladle out some of the juices. Put in a pan over a low heat and stir in the thickening granules until dissolved and the sauce is thickened. Add the sauce and peas back into the slow cooker and stir to thicken. Season with salt and pepper, and leave for 10 mins to heat through. Stir in chopped mint and garnish with a few mint leaves just before serving.

MAIN MEALS

Lamb with peppers, dates and chickpeas

Use best end of neck chops for a super-tender result with heaps of flavour that also comes in at a great price

Serves 6 • Ready in 6 hrs

- 1kg (2lb) lamb neck chops
- 3tbsp olive oil
- 1 large onion, finely chopped
- 2 red peppers, sliced
- 4 garlic cloves, crushed
- 1tsp ground coriander
- 1tsp ground cumin
- 1tsp cinnamon
- ½tsp ground ginger
- 400g (14oz) tin chopped tomatoes
- 500ml (17fl oz) beef stock
- 2tbsp tomato purée
- 75g (2.5oz) pitted dates, roughly chopped
- 2 x 400g (14oz) tins chickpeas, drained and rinsed
- 2tbsp chopped fresh parsley
- Crusty bread, to serve

1 Season the chops with salt and pepper. Heat the oil in a large frying pan over a high heat, and fry the lamb in batches for 5 mins until browned.
2 Add the meat, along with the onion, peppers, garlic, spices, tomatoes, stock, tomato purée, dates and chickpeas to the slow cooker.
3 Cook on low for 6 hrs or until the lamb is tender and falling from the bone. Plate up, scatter over the parsley and serve with crusty bread.

Cook's Tip
If you're extra hungry, serve with mashed potatoes.

MAIN MEALS

Cook once, eat twice
Make this tasty, tagine and serve half with couscous. Freeze the rest to make pasties later.

Minty lamb & feta pasties

Use your slow cooker lamb tagine to make a lunctime treat

Serves 4 • Ready in 20 mins

Defrost lamb mixture in the fridge the day before you need it. Heat oven to 200°C/400°F/Gas 6. Mix lamb with 100g (3.5oz) feta, crumbled, and 1½tsp mint sauce. Unroll 375g (13oz) pack ready-rolled shortcrust pastry. Cut out 4 x 18cm (1.5 x 7in) circles, brush edges with egg wash from 1 egg, beaten. Divide filling between the 4 circles, fold up edges and crimp. Brush with egg and sprinkle with black pepper. Bake for 20 mins until golden and piping hot.

MAIN MEALS

Spiced lamb tagine

Perfect served with healthy couscous and a great way to use up leftover lamb

Serves 4 • Ready in 5 hrs 20 mins

- 700g (1lb 9oz) stewing lamb, cut into chunks
- 1tbsp olive oil
- 1 large onion, chopped
- 3 sticks celery, diced
- 3 carrots, diced
- 3tsp harissa paste
- 1tsp each ground cumin and coriander
- 150g (5oz) dried apricots, chopped
- 200ml (7fl oz) hot lamb stock
- 560g (20oz) bottle passata
- 400g (14oz) tin chickpeas, drained
- 290g (10oz) jar roasted peppers in brine, drained and chopped
- 4 large strips lemon zest
- Handful of parsley, chopped
- Handful of cashews
- 400g (14oz) cooked couscous

1 Heat a large deep frying pan. In batches, brown lamb. Set aside. Heat olive oil and cook onion, celery, and carrots for 5 mins. Add to the slow cooker.
2 Stir in harissa paste, cumin and coriander, dried apricots and hot lamb stock. Cook for 4-5 hrs on low until lamb is tender, then season.
3 Set aside half mixture, chill, then freeze for up to 3 months for your pasties. To the remaining lamb, add passata, chickpeas, roasted peppers and lemon zest. Simmer for 15 mins on the hob, stir in handful parsley, chopped. Sprinkle with cashews and serve with couscous.

"The baharat-spiced lamb also works well in flatbreads"

Lamb pittas

Treat yourself to a posh kebab with these warming Middle Eastern flavours

Serves 4 • Ready in 4 hrs

- 2 lamb necks (approx 225g/8oz total)
- 1-2tsp baharat spice blend
- 2tsp vegetable oil
- 60ml (2fl oz) water
- 4 pittas
- 4 tomatoes, sliced
- ½ cucumber, thinly sliced
- 1 small red onion, peeled and thinly sliced

For the sauce
- 1tbsp tahini
- 1tbsp fat-free Greek yoghurt
- ½ lemon juice

1 Season the lamb necks and rub in the spice. Heat up the oil in a frying pan and brown the lamb for 2 mins on each side. Cook with 60ml (2fl oz) water for 4 hrs on low in the slow cooker.
2 Mix the sauce ingredients and season to taste.
3 Grill the pitta then open and spoon in some of the sauce. Fill with the tomato, cucumber, meat, onion, then a little more tahini sauce.

The Ultimate Slow Cooker Cookbook

MAIN MEALS

Cook's Tip
You don't have to squeeze the sausages out of the skins — just blitz them in a food processor as they are.

Surprise sausage bolognese

A tasty twist on everyone's favourite pasta dish, using sausages and plenty of hidden veg. Ideal for fussy eaters!

Serves 4 • Ready in 6-8 hrs

- 1 carrot, roughly chopped
- 1 celery stick, cut into 4
- 4 spring onions, trimmed
- 2 garlic cloves, peeled
- 400g (14oz) sausages
- 1tbsp olive oil
- 400g (14oz) tin tomatoes
- 400g (14oz) water
- 4tbsp balsamic vinegar
- 350g (12oz) pappardelle
- 2tbsp freshly grated Parmesan
- Basil leaves, to serve

1 Put the carrot, celery, spring onions and garlic into a food processor and blitz to finely chop. Add the sausages and blend again to a mince texture.
2 Heat the oil in a frying pan over a medium heat. Tip in the sausage mix and cook for 10 mins, stirring, until it breaks up.
3 Add to the slow cooker, along with the tomatoes, vinegar and water. Cook for 6-8 hrs on low.
4 In the last 20-30 mins, add the pasta to the slow cooker, stir and cook until al dente. Season to taste and serve with grated Parmesan and a scattering of basil leaves.

"You can use pork, beef, chicken or vegetarian sausages for this dish and any type of pasta"

Sweet miso pork

Slow-cooked with a glaze that makes it sweet, sour and deliciously sticky

Serves 6 • Prep 10 mins • Cook 6 hrs 15 mins

- 1.2-1.5kg (3lb) pork shoulder, boned and rolled, skin scored

For the glaze
- 250g (9oz) pack sweet white miso paste
- 50ml (1fl oz) soy sauce
- 100g (3.5oz) runny honey
- 75ml (2.5fl oz) mirin (Japanese rice wine)

1 Turn your slow cooker on to low to heat up. To make the glaze, mix all the ingredients together in a bowl until well combined.
2 Pour the miso glaze into the slow cooker and place the meat in it. Then brush the glaze all over the meat. Cook on low for 6 hrs, until super tender, glazing the meat every hour or so.
3 Turn the oven up to 200°C/400°F/Gas 6. If you want crackling, once the pork is cooked, slice off the top layer of fat and put it in the oven until the skin starts to crackle, then brush the crackling with a little glaze before serving. Cut into thick slices and serve with mash or rice and stir-fried greens.

MAIN MEALS

Cook's Tip
You'll have more glaze than you need, but it keeps in the fridge and is great with chicken or as a stirfry sauce.

MAIN MEALS

Pork with Bramley apple and tarragon

Think of this as pork in apple sauce, which is not too sweet! This makes a large quantity so you can freeze half

Serves 8-10 • Ready in 2 hrs 30 mins

- Oil, for frying
- 2kg (4lb) pork shoulder or leg, cut into chunks
- 1 large onion, chopped
- 2tbsp seasoned flour
- 2 Bramley apples, peeled, cored and chopped
- 500ml (16fl oz) dry cider
- 1 bunch of tarragon, leaves chopped
- 3tbsp crème fraîche or double cream

1 Heat the oil in a large pan, then brown the meat in batches. Set aside. Add a little more oil and gently cook the onion until soft. Return the pork to the same pan and add the flour. Stir well for a few mins, then add the apples and cider. Transfer to your slow cooker and cook on low for 2 hrs 30 mins.
2 Add the tarragon and crème fraîche and serve.

Slow-braised spicy pork and prunes

Pomegranate molasses is a rich source of anti-ageing nutrients

Serves 6 to 8 •
Ready in 3 hrs 35 mins

- 4tbsp olive oil
- 1.5kg (3lb 6oz) boneless shoulder or leg of pork, trimmed of excess fat and cut into 10cm (4in) chunks
- 2 onions, peeled and sliced
- 3 garlic cloves, peeled and crushed
- 2 red chillies, deseeded and chopped
- 4cm (1.5in) piece root ginger, grated
- Large bunch coriander
- 1tsp each fennel seeds and sumac
- 2tsp ground cumin
- ½tsp ground coriander
- ¼tsp ground cloves
- 1l (1.75pt) chicken stock
- 50ml (2fl oz) lemon juice
- 250g (9oz) soft dried prunes
- 2tbsp each pomegranate molasses, maple syrup and tamari or soy sauce

1 In a large frying pan, heat the oil. Fry the pork in batches until well browned. Remove to a plate. Add the onions to the pan and fry gently until soft. Add the garlic, chillies, ginger, coriander stalks and fennel seeds, and fry for 2 mins. Add the sumac, cumin, ground coriander and cloves, plus 100ml (4fl oz) water, and cook gently for 5 mins, stirring. Then, add to the slow cooker.
2 Pour in the stock and lemon juice, stir well, and add the pork to the slow cooker. Cover and cook for 3 hrs, stirring occasionally.
3 Remove the pork from the slow cooker. Add the prunes to a pan on low heat, along with the liquid in the slow cooker. Stir in the molasses, maple syrup and tamari, and simmer to reduce by half.
4 Shred the meat, season, then return to the juices. Serve with couscous. Can be frozen for up to 2 months.

MAIN MEALS

Pork chops with tomato and fennel sauce

Pork shoulder chops work well here, as they are better suited to a slow cook than loin chops

Serves 4 • Prep 15 mins • Cook 6-8 hrs

- 4 pork shoulder chops (approx 800g/1lb 12oz)
- 4tbsp extra virgin olive oil
- 1 small onion, chopped
- 1 small head fennel, trimmed and chopped
- 2 garlic cloves, crushed
- 1kg (2lb) ripe vine tomatoes, chopped, or 2 x 400g (14oz) tins chopped tomatoes
- 1tsp grated lemon zest
- 1tsp caster sugar
- 2 sprigs fresh sage, bruised
- 2 bay leaves, bruised
- 150g (5oz) orzo pasta
- 1tbsp basil leaves
- Freshly grated Parmesan, to serve

1 Season the chops with salt and pepper. Heat half the oil in a large frying pan and brown the chops on both sides for 3-4 mins. Remove and set aside.
2 Add the remaining oil to the pan and gently fry the onion, fennel and garlic for 10 mins until really soft but not browned.
3 Add, along with the pork, tomatoes, lemon zest, caster sugar, sage and bay leaves, to the slow cooker. Cook on low for 6-8 hrs, stirring occasionally, until tender.
3 In the last 20-30 mins stir in the orzo and cook. Plate up, scatter over the basil leaves and serve with grated Parmesan.

Cook's Tip
If you prefer, use a grain such as farro instead of the orzo.

MAIN MEALS

MAIN MEALS

Cook's Tip
Different rub brands may vary (try Bart Smokehouse Barbecue Chipotle Rub).

Pulled pork

A slow-cooking winner — the prep only takes 5 mins, then can be left to cook all day

Serves 6 • Ready in 6-8 hrs

- 1.5kg (3lb) boneless pork shoulder
- 1 pack chipotle barbecue rub (see tip)
- 1tsp coarse black pepper
- 1tbsp oil
- 8tbsp ketchup
- 4tbsp cider vinegar
- 2tbsp Worcestershire sauce
- 1tbsp honey, or low-carb alternative
- 150ml (5fl oz) beef or pork stock
- Coleslaw and rocket, to serve
- 1 small bunch fresh coriander, roughly chopped, to garnish

1 Turn the slow cooker to high and rub the pork all over with the chipotle mix, black pepper and oil. Place in the slow cooker with the ketchup, vinegar, Worcestershire sauce, honey and stock. Cover and cook for 6-8 hrs.
2 When the pork is done, put the cooked meat onto a chopping board and, using 2 forks, shred the meat into small pieces. Stir the shredded meat back into the cooking juices, which should have reduced to a thick sauce. Serve the meat with coleslaw and a rocket salad, garnished with some fresh coriander.

Chinese spiced pork belly with plums

This dish is a good way to make the most of tasty, but great-value, pork

Serves 8 • Ready in 3-6 hrs

- 1.25kg (2lb 12oz) pork belly, cut into slices
- 2 cinnamon sticks
- 3 star anise
- 1tsp Chinese five spice
- 6 plums, halved
- 150ml (5fl oz) red wine
- Juice of 2 oranges
- 1 chicken stock pot
- 150g (5oz) Chinese greens, such as pak choi or tatsoi

1 Put the pork into a slow cooker with the cinnamon, star anise, five spice, plums, wine, orange juice and stock pot. Cook on low for 6 hrs or high for 3 hrs.
2 Skim off the fat, add the Chinese greens so that the stalks are immersed and allow to steam for two to three minutes. Serve with mixed vegetables or cauliflower rice.

"The spice from the cinnamon and sweetness of the plums work wonders with the pork"

MAIN MEALS

Cook's Tip
If you have any leftovers, store in an airtight container in the fridge and use within a few days.

MAIN MEALS

MAIN MEALS

Smoky pork and Boston beans one pot

An easy one-pot dinner that everyone will love

Serves 6 • Ready in 4 hrs 15 mins

- 600g (1lb 5oz) pork shoulder steaks
- 1tbsp New York Steak Rub (we used Bart)
- 2tbsp olive oil
- 2 garlic cloves, crushed
- 4tbsp red wine vinegar
- 1tbsp light muscovado sugar
- 400g (14oz) tin cherry tomatoes
- 1tsp chipotle paste
- 1 chicken stock pot
- 2 x 400g (14oz) tins cannellini beans
- A few leaves of flat-leaf parsley
- Garlic bread, to serve

1 Heat a slow cooker. Put the pork into a shallow dish and sprinkle over the steak rub.
2 Heat the oil in a large frying pan, add the pork and cook for a few mins, to brown. Add along with the garlic, vinegar, sugar, tomatoes, paste, stock pot and 150ml (5fl oz) water to the slow cooker. Cook on low for 4 hrs.
3 Stir in the beans and warm through. Sprinkle over the parsley and serve with garlic bread.

"Freeze any filling you don't need – it's delicious in a jacket potato"

Slow winter cottage pie

This twist on a classic winter warmer makes a large quantity to save time and money on fuel bills

Serves 10-12 • Ready in 4 hrs 30 mins

- 1tbsp oil
- 1kg (2lb) pork shoulder, cut into cubes
- 1kg (2lb) beef shin, cut into cubes
- 3 medium onions, peeled and chopped
- 2 sticks of celery, chopped
- 2tbsp seasoned flour
- 500g (1lb) Chantenay carrots, trimmed
- 3 garlic cloves, crushed
- ½tbsp coriander seeds, crushed
- ¾tsp sweet smoked paprika
- 500ml (17fl oz) red wine
- 1 Knorr Vegetable Stock Pot
- 2 x 400g (14oz) tins chopped tomatoes
- 4tbsp Worcestershire sauce
- 2 x 400g (14oz) packs of ready-made mashed potato (or homemade)
- 50g (2oz) mature Cheddar, finely grated
- 2tbsp dried breadcrumbs

1 Heat the oil in a large frying pan. Brown the meat in batches and set aside. Cook the onions and celery in the same pan for 5 mins or until starting to brown. Stir in the flour.
2 Add the onion mixture, along with the meat, carrots, garlic, coriander seeds and paprika to the slow cooker. Pour in the red wine, stock pot, tomatoes and Worcestershire sauce and stir. Cook for 3 hours 30 mins on low or until very tender. Season well. You can freeze it now or store for 2-3 days in the fridge.
3 Heat the oven to 180°C/350°F/Gas 4. Fill an ovenproof dish with around three-quarters of the mixture (freeze the leftovers) and top with the mash, covering evenly. Sprinkle over the cheese and breadcrumbs and cook for 30-40 mins or until bubbling and browned.

MAIN MEALS

MAIN MEALS

Spring pork and cider casserole

A quick one-pot with zesty, punchy flavours. Serve with a crunchy salad

Serves 4 • Ready in 6-8 hrs

- 1tbsp olive oil
- 600g (1lb 5oz) pork loin fillet, sliced into medallions
- 1 red onion, thinly sliced
- 2 garlic cloves, grated
- 2tsp fennel seeds
- 500ml (1pt) low-carb cider
- 3tbsp crème fraîche
- 75g (2.5oz) mixed pitted olives
- 3tbsp capers
- Zest and juice of 2 lemons
- A large handful of parsley, chopped

1 Heat the oil in a heavy-based frying pan and fry the pork in batches for two mins on each side, until browned and almost cooked through. Set aside.
2 Gently cook the onion with the garlic and fennel seeds until the onion has softened. Add to slow cooker, pour over the cider and cook for 6-8 hrs on low, until the pork is tender.
3 Stir through the crème fraîche, olives, capers, lemon zest and juice. Season and scatter with parsley to serve.

Cook's Tip
This also works really well with chicken legs or thighs.

"Serve with creamy mash potatoes and seasonal greens for a hearty, winter meal"

MAIN MEALS

Ropa Vieja

Tender and tasty, this slow-cooked Cuban stew is worth waiting for

Serves 6-8 • Ready in 8 hrs

- 1.1kg (2.5lb) flank or chuck steak
- Salt and pepper, for seasoning
- 3tbsp vegetable oil
- 1 large onion, chopped
- 1 red pepper, thinly sliced
- 1 yellow or green bell pepper, thinly sliced
- 6 cloves garlic, minced
- 800g (28oz) tinned tomatoes
- 250ml (9fl oz) white wine
- 1tsp dried oregano
- 1tsp ground cumin
- 1tsp paprika
- 90g (3oz) green olives, halved
- 540g (19oz) white rice
- 1 small handful coriander (cilantro), chopped

1 Pat the steak dry and season well with salt and pepper.
3 Heat the oil in a large frying pan over a medium-high heat and cook the steak for 5-8 mins until browned on both sides. Set the steak aside.
4 Fry off the onion and garlic.
5 Add the steak, onion and garlic, peppers, tomatoes, white wine, oregano and spices to the slow cooker.
7 Cook on low for around 8 hrs, until the meat is very tender.
8 In the last 20 mins of cooking time, remove the steaks from the slow cooker and use a couple of forks to pull the meat it into thin shreds.
9 Return the beef to the stew, add the olives, season to taste and cook for the last 20 mins until the meat is coated with a thick sauce.
10 Meanwhile, cook the rice in a pan or rice cooker.
11 Serve the ropa vieja over rice and top with the coriander.

Beef chilli and black beans

Take this old favourite to a new level with tender chunks of slow-cooked beef and smoky ancho chillies

Serves 4 • Ready in 4-8 hrs

- 2 dried ancho chillies
- 1 dried chipotle chilli (or a good pinch of flaked chipotle)
- 400ml (13.5fl oz) beef stock
- 2-3tbsp sunflower oil
- 500g (1lb) beef stewing steak, cut into large chunks
- 1 red onion, peeled and chopped
- 1 stick celery, chopped
- 2 garlic cloves, crushed
- 1-2 red chillies, sliced
- 1tsp ground cumin
- 1tsp smoked paprika
- 1 cinnamon stick
- 400g (14oz) tin chopped tomatoes
- 1tbsp tomato purée
- 400g (14oz) tin black beans, drained and rinsed
- A little brown sugar

1 Soak the dried chillies in a large jug with the hot beef stock and set aside.
2 Heat a little oil in a large frying pan. Brown the beef in batches and place at the bottom of your slow cooker. Add the onions and celery.
3 Remove the hydrated chillies from the stock and slice. Add to the slow cooker with the garlic, fresh chillies, spices and beef.
4 Pour over the stock, tomatoes, purée and beans. Stir well to mix. Cook for 4 hrs on high, or 8 hrs on low.
5 For the final 30 mins of cooking time remove the slow cooker lid to reduce the liquid. Alternatively, transfer the chilli to a saucepan and reduce on the hob on a low heat. Add sugar and seasoning to taste.
6 Serve with rice, sour cream and guacamole.

MAIN MEALS

MAIN MEALS

Pulled beef ragu

If you like a meaty pasta dish, you'll love this tender version in a rich wine sauce

Serves 4 • Ready in 6 hrs

- 800g (1lb 12oz) beef shin or brisket
- 2 carrots, roughly chopped
- 1 stick celery, roughly chopped
- 1 bay leaf
- 4 garlic cloves, bashed
- 250ml (9fl oz) red wine
- 1 beef stock pot, we used Knorr
- 4tbsp tomato purée
- Cooked pasta and fresh basil, to serve
- 50g (2oz) Parmesan, grated

1 Put the beef, vegetables, bay leaf, garlic, wine, stock, 200ml (7fl oz) water and the tomato purée into a slow cooker and season. Cook on low for 6 hrs.
2 Remove the meat to a board and pull the strands apart using two forks. Meanwhile, put the pot on the hob and reduce the sauce until thickened to your liking. Check the seasoning, then put the meat back in the pot and mix together with the sauce.
3 Cook some pasta according to pack instructions. Serve with the pasta and a sprinkling of Parmesan and basil.

MAIN MEALS

Pot roast beef brisket

Retro beef brisket is not only a cheaper cut of meat, but it is perfect for a Sunday roast

Serves 4-6 • Ready in 5 hrs

- 1.8kg (4lb) boned and rolled brisket of beef
- 4-6 garlic cloves, peeled and thinly sliced
- 3tbsp olive oil
- 12 shallots (400g/14oz), peeled
- 75g (2.5oz) diced pancetta
- 1 large carrot, peeled and diced
- 3 celery sticks – 1 finely chopped, 2 cut into 5cm (2in) lengths
- 1 x 75cl (25fl oz) bottle red wine
- A few sprigs of thyme
- 2-3 bay leaves
- 2tbsp tomato purée/ketchup
- 1tsp muscovado sugar
- About 300g (10.5oz) Chantenay or young carrots

1 Make deep cuts in the beef and push garlic slivers down inside. Season the meat.
2 Heat 1tbsp oil in a large frying pan and brown the meat all over. Put in a warmed slow-cook pot. Add 1tbsp oil to the pan with the shallots and brown them. Set aside in a bowl. Reduce the heat and cook the pancetta, diced carrot and celery for 5 mins.
3 Pour in the wine, add the thyme, bay leaves, tomato purée/ketchup and sugar. Bring to a simmer and pour over the beef in the slow cooker pot. Cover and cook on high for 4 hrs or low for 2 hrs.
4 Add the shallots, carrot and rest of the celery. Cover and cook for another 2-3 hrs on low or 1 hr on high, until the meat is tender.
5 Put meat on a serving platter with the vegetables, cover with foil and leave to rest for 10 mins. Boil the cooking juices in a pan to reduce and thicken. Season. Serve the meat, along with the mashed potatoes and wedges of cabbage.

Cook's Tip
To make shallots easier to peel, put them in a pan, cover with cold water, bring to the boil and simmer for 5 mins. Cool them under cold running water and peel.

MAIN MEALS

Cook's Tip
Feel free to mix and match which vegetables you use in this recipe.

MAIN MEALS

Steak fajitas

Use your favourite cut of steak for this update on the Mexican classic

Serves 2 • Ready in 4-8 hrs

- 2tbsp olive oil
- 2 mixed peppers, cut into strips
- 1 large red onion, sliced
- 500g (1lb) skirt or chuck steak
- 2 garlic cloves, finely chopped
- 1tsp ground cumin
- 1½tsp ground coriander
- ½tsp hot chilli powder
- 100ml (3.5fl oz) water
- 2 tomatoes, chopped
- Handful of chopped coriander
- Wraps, warmed

To serve:
- Yoghurt, cheese and guacamole

1 In a frying pan, add 1tbsp olive oil and brown your cut of steak before transferring to the slow cooker.
2 Add the second tbsp of olive oil and soften the onions, peppers and garlic. Transfer to the slow cooker along with the chopped tomatoes.
3 Mix together the cumin, coriander and chilli powder with the water to form a seasoning stock. Pour into the slow cooker, replace the lid and cook on high for 4 hrs, or low for 8 hrs.
4 Once cooked, remove the steak from the slow cooker, slice, return it to the slow cooker and mix with the vegetables. Serve in the wraps with chopped coriander alongside yoghurt, cheese and guacamole.

"Why not roll up your tortillas, top with cheese and put under the grill?"

MAIN MEALS

Beef short rib and leek hot pot

Try this rich and decadent autumn dinner that's sure to please a crowd

Serves 6 •
Ready in 8 hrs 20 mins

For the beef ribs:
- 1tbsp olive oil
- 4 beef short ribs
- 2 red onions, sliced into rings
- 4 garlic cloves, crushed
- 500ml (17fl oz) beef stock
- 3 tbsp Worcestershire sauce

For the hot pot:
- 60g (2oz) butter
- 1tbsp extra virgin olive oil
- 400g (14oz) leeks, sliced
- 1 onion, chopped
- 2 garlic cloves
- 750g (26oz) waxy potatoes, sliced
- 1 tsp thyme leaves
- 60g (2.5oz) grated raclette cheese

1 For the ribs, heat the oil in a large frying pan. Season the beef and fry with the onions and garlic, turning as needed, for 5 mins.
2 Tip into a slow cooker. Add the stock and Worcestershire sauce. Cover and cook for 6 hrs on low.
3 For the hot pot, heat half the butter with the oil and fry the leeks and onion, stirring well. Add the garlic, cook for 1 min, cover the casserole and cook for 10 mins, then remove.
4 Put half the potatoes into the casserole. Season. Remove the meat from the ribs and shred. Pile on top of the potatoes. Spoon on the leek mixture. Arrange a layer of potatoes on top and pour in the stock. Season and sprinkle with thyme and cheese.
5 Cover, then oven-cook the hot pot for 1 hr 30 mins.
6 Remove the lid, dot the potatoes with the rest of the butter and cook uncovered for 30 mins, until it is golden on top.

Beef rogan josh

Serve this hearty Indian stew to friends and family to warm them up as the weather gets colder

Serves 8 •
Ready in 3 hrs 30 mins

- 900g (2lb) stewing beef, cut into 3cm (1.75in) cubes
- 2tbsp vegetable oil
- 2 white onions, finely sliced
- 1 thumb-sized piece of root ginger, peeled and grated
- 3 garlic cloves, puréed
- 1tsp garam masala
- 280g (10oz) rogan josh curry paste
- 1tbsp tomato purée
- 750ml (25fl oz) hot beef stock
- 500g (1lb) sweet potato, peeled and cut into 2cm (0.75in) cubes
- Small bunch of fresh coriander, finely chopped
- 1 red onion, finely sliced

1 Switch the slow cooker on high and pour in the 2 tbsp of oil.
2 Add the onions, garlic, ginger, garam masala, rogan josh paste, tomato purée, sweet potatoes and beef.
3 Pour in the hot beef stock and give it a good stir.
4 Cook for 3 hrs 30 mins until the beef is tender. To serve, top with the coriander and red onion.

MAIN MEALS

Cook's Tip
Cook up a couple of extra beef ribs one day, then make the hot pot the following day.

MAIN MEALS

Chiang Mai beef curry

This classic and easy Thai dish is just 245 calories per serving, so you can enjoy it guilt-free

Serves 4 • Ready in 1 hr

- 8 baby sweetcorn, halved
- 150g (5oz) green beans
- 1tbsp vegetable oil
- 1 onion, chopped
- 2 garlic cloves, puréed
- 2tbsp yellow Thai curry paste
- 350g (12oz) sirloin steak, fat trimmed, cut into strips
- 1 red pepper, deseeded, sliced
- 8 kaffir lime leaves
- 1tsp brown sugar
- 2tbsp black bean sauce
- 100ml (3.5fl oz) water
- Juice of 1 lime
- 4tsp Thai fish sauce
- 12 Thai basil leaves
- 8 mint leaves, sliced

1 Plunge the sweetcorn and green beans into a pan of boiling water for 2 mins to soften slightly, then drain.
2 Switch the slow cooker on high and add 1tbsp of vegetable oil.
3 Add the onions, garlic, Thai curry paste, pepper, beans, sweetcorn, lime juice, sugar, black bean sauce, lime leaves, fish sauce and 100ml (3.5fl oz) of water and give it a good stir.
4 Cook for 1 hr on high. Serve straight away tossed with your favourite noodles or rice.

Cook's Tip
If you don't have fish sauce, use 3-4tsp soy sauce and a little extra sugar to taste.

MAIN MEALS

Rich beef rendang

This classic slow-cooked Indonesian curry is full of flavour with its rich, melt-in-the-mouth beef

Serves 6 • Ready in 6 hrs 30 mins

For the rendang curry paste:
- 80g (3oz) toasted desiccated coconut
- 1tbsp coriander seeds
- 10 dried bird's-eye chillies, soaked in hot water
- 3 shallots, roughly chopped
- 4 garlic cloves, peeled
- 1tbsp galangal paste
- Thumb-sized piece fresh ginger, peeled and roughly chopped
- 1 heaped tsp ground turmeric
- 2 stalks lemongrass, white part only, sliced
- 6 kaffir lime leaves, stalks removed
- 1tbsp dark brown sugar
- 2tbsp vegetable oil

For the curry:
- 1tbsp vegetable oil
- 1 cinnamon stick
- 3-4 cardamom pods, crushed
- 2 cloves
- 3tbsp tamarind paste
- 30g (1oz) dark brown sugar
- 1.5kg (3lb) stewing beef
- 800ml (27fl oz) coconut milk
- 2tbsp fish sauce
- Juice of 2 limes
- Small bunch fresh coriander
- Chopped red chilli, to garnish

1 Add 40g (1.5oz) of the toasted coconut, along with the other curry paste ingredients, to a food processor and blitz until smooth.
2 In a frying pan, heat the vegetable oil and add in the curry paste, along with the cinnamon stick, cardamom and cloves. Cook over a medium-high heat for 5 mins before adding the tamarind paste and sugar. Add the beef and cook until browned.
3 Add to the slow cooker, along with the coconut milk, fish sauce and lime juice. Cook for 6 hrs on high.
4 After 6 hrs, check the consistency, add a splash of water if needed and cook for a further 30 mins. To freeze ahead, leave to cool completely, place in a freezable container and freeze for up to 3 months. Defrost completely in the fridge before heating through (you may want to add a couple of tbsp of water before reheating).
5 Scatter with fresh coriander and chilli and the remaining coconut. Serve with rice.

Cook's Tip
Rendang is a dark, rich dish, but to make it a little lighter, swap one of the tins of coconut milk for a reduced-fat version.

"Rendang curry can also be made with leftover beef from your Sunday roast"

MAIN MEALS

Beef bourguignon

Our version of the classic dish has all the usual richness of flavour, but can be made with less time in the kitchen

Serves 2-3 • Ready in 4-8 hrs

- 1tbsp olive oil
- 200g (7oz) baby chestnut mushrooms
- 1 onion, finely chopped
- 65g (2.5oz) diced pancetta
- 3 garlic cloves, crushed
- 3 shallots, halved
- 100ml (3.5oz) beef stock
- 375ml (12fl oz) red wine
- 1tbsp plain flour
- 1 bouquet garni
- 10g (0.5oz) butter
- 500g (1lb) diced beef
- 1 stick celery, chopped
- 1 carrot, roughly chopped
- Chopped parsley, to garnish
- Steamed Tenderstem broccoli, to serve (optional)

1 In a large frying pan, heat the olive oil and butter together. Add the pancetta and fry for 2 mins until pancetta releases its fats. Using a slotted spoon, transfer the pancetta to the slow cooker, leaving the oils in the pan.
2 Coat the diced beef in the flour, mixed with a generous pinch of salt and pepper, and then brown the meat in the remaining fat in the saucepan. Transfer the browned meat to the slow cooker.
3 Add onion, garlic, celery, carrot, shallots and baby chestnut mushrooms to the slow cooker, followed by the red wine and beef stock.
4 Add the thyme and bay leaf and place the lid on the slow cooker, leaving to cook for 4 hrs on high or 8 hrs on low.
5 Half an hour before serving, remove the slow cooker lid to reduce the liquid. Alternatively, transfer the bourguignon to a saucepan and reduce on the hob on a low heat. Remove the bouquet garni and serve with mashed potatoes and chopped parsley.

"This also pairs well with crusty bread if you are short on time"

MAIN MEALS

MAIN MEALS

Cook's Tip

Coconut chutney: In a food processor, whizz 100g (3.5oz) fresh coconut; 1 green chilli, chopped; 2cm (1in) piece ginger, grated; handful coriander leaves; and zest and juice 1 lime.

MAIN MEALS

Beef curry with fresh coconut chutney

Rich and meaty, with beef so tender you can cut it with a spoon. This easy, make-ahead number will liberate you from the stove

**Serves 8-10 •
Ready in 4 hrs 30 mins**

- 1tbsp peanut or vegetable oil
- 1.5kg (3lb) beef cheek or shin, cut into 6cm (2.5in) pieces
- 1 cinnamon stick
- 3 star anise
- 4 cardamom pods, bashed
- 1 stick lemongrass, pressed with the flat side of a knife to release the flavour
- 4 fresh lime leaves, bashed (or 8 dried)
- 160ml (5.5fl oz) coconut cream
- 200ml (7fl oz) rich beef stock
- 100g (3.5oz) peanut butter
- 2tbsp dark brown sugar
- 2tbsp tamarind paste
- 2tbsp ketjap manis (or use soy and a little more sugar)
- 2tbsp fish sauce
- 500g (1lb) potatoes, peeled, cut into 5cm (2in) pieces

To serve:
Roti or rice, crispy fried shallots, roasted peanuts, coriander leaves and lime wedges
Coconut chutney (see Cook's tip)

For the curry paste:
- 2 banana shallots, chopped
- 5 garlic cloves, bashed
- 2 red chillies, roughly chopped, plus extra cut into fine strips, to serve
- 5cm (2in) piece fresh ginger, finely chopped, plus extra cut into fine strips, to serve
- Juice 2 limes, plus extra to season
- 1tbsp lemongrass paste
- 1tbsp ground cumin
- 1tsp ground nutmeg
- ½tsp ground cloves

1 Put the curry paste ingredients into a small food processor and whizz until finely chopped.
2 Heat the oil in a large, heavy-based saucepan over a medium-high heat. Season the beef with salt and cook in batches until well browned all over. Add to the slow cooker, along with the whole spices, lemongrass and lime leaves.
3 Add the remaining ingredients, except for the potatoes and cook on high for 4 hrs, adding the potatoes in for the final hr of cooking time.
4 Taste the sauce and adjust the seasoning with more fish sauce, sugar or lime juice as liked.
5 Meanwhile, to make the chutney, whizz all the ingredients together in a small food processor until finely chopped. Season with salt, then set aside.
6 Serve the curry with roti or rice, and top with the crispy fried shallots, roasted peanuts, sliced chilli and ginger, coriander leaves, lime wedges and the coconut chutney.

Beef and sweet potato stew

Minced beef is made more tasty by adding sweet potatoes and celery

**Serves 4 •
Ready in 5 hrs 10 mins**

- 1tbsp sunflower oil
- 1 onion, chopped
- 500g (1lb) minced beef
- 1 large carrot, chopped
- 2 celery sticks, chopped
- 400g (14oz) tin chopped tomatoes
- 2tsp sun-dried tomato paste
- 1tbsp Worcestershire sauce
- 600ml (20fl oz) beef stock
- 500g (1lb) sweet potatoes, peeled and cubed
- Flat-leaf parsley, to serve

1 Heat a slow cooker. Heat the oil in a large pan and fry the onion gently for a few mins, to soften. Add the mince, season and cook for 10 mins, turning as needed until browned.
2 Add the carrot, celery, tomatoes, tomato paste, Worcestershire sauce, stock and sweet potatoes. Bring to the boil, then add the mixture to the slow cooker.
3 Cook on low for 5 hrs. Serve sprinkled with flat-leaf parsley leaves to finish.

MAIN MEALS

MAIN MEALS

Spanish oxtail stew with chorizo

All the flavours of the Med are in this delicious dish!

Serves 6 • Ready in 6 hrs 10 mins

- 3tbsp olive oil
- 1.2kg (2.6lb) oxtail (ask your butcher to cut it into 2.5cm/1in slices)
- 200g (7oz) cooking chorizo sausages
- 1tbsp steak seasoning
- 2tsp smoked paprika
- 2 onions, sliced
- 3 garlic cloves, crushed
- 150ml (5fl oz) balsamic vinegar
- 500ml (17oz) beef stock
- 800g (28oz) cherry tomatoes
- Few sprigs of rosemary
- 500g (17oz) Chantenay carrots, halved
- 400g (14oz) butter beans
- Savoy cabbage, sliced to serve

1 Heat half the olive oil in a large frying pan and fry the oxtail and chorizo with the steak seasoning and paprika for 5 mins to brown evenly. Remove and reserve.
2 Heat the rest of the oil and fry the onion and garlic for a few mins until softened, but not browned.
3 Tip the oxtail, chorizo, vinegar, stock, tomatoes, rosemary and carrots into the slow cooker. Cover and cook for 6 hrs, until the meat is really tender.
4 If using the butter beans, drain, tip in and warm through. Serve with stir-fried savoy cabbage.

Cook's Tip
Prepare this dish up to the end of step 3, then freeze. Reheat and continue from step 4.

MAIN MEALS

Cook's Tip
Buy 1kg (2lb) packs of frozen squid and keep the rest in the freezer for quick stir-fry meals. They thaw quickly.

Spanish-style squid

Squid is a relatively inexpensive seafood and delicious when cooked slowly, making it soft and tender

Serves 4-6 • Ready in 3 hrs

- 600g (1.25lb) squid (16-20 of them), cleaned and cut into 2.5cm (1in) pieces
- 1 large onion, peeled and cut into wedges
- 4 fat garlic cloves, unpeeled
- 6 large ripe tomatoes, skinned, quartered and deseeded
- 2 x 400g (14oz) tins chickpeas, rinsed and drained
- 2 bay leaves, torn
- 1tsp smoked paprika
- 2tbsp good olive oil
- 200ml (7fl oz) Fino or Amontillado sherry
- 200g (7oz) chorizo ring, sliced thickly
- Good pinch of saffron threads
- 1tsp whole black peppercorns
- 1tbsp finely chopped mint
- 2tbsp finely chopped parsley
- Crusty bread and salad/greens, to serve

1 Heat the oil over a low heat and fry the onion and garlic for 5 mins. Add to the slow cooker.
2 Put the squid, tomato, chorizo, chickpeas, bay leaves, paprika, oil, sherry and 300ml (½pt) water into the slow cooker. Cook on high for 3 hrs. Add more water if the sauce is getting too thick.
3 Meanwhile, toast the saffron threads in a small, dry frying pan over a medium heat, until they darken. Put them in a mortar with the peppercorns and grind to a powder with the pestle. Add to the slow cooker while cooking.
3 Stir in the herbs. Serve hot with the crusty bread and salad.

Prawn and squash curry

When curry cravings strike, this balti curry with pink, juicy prawns will hit the spot

Serves 4 • Ready in 1 hr 35 mins

- 3tbsp balti curry paste
- 1 medium butternut squash, cut into chunks
- 400g (14oz) tin reduced-fat coconut milk
- 400g (14oz) bag frozen peeled prawns
- A few sprigs of basil, roughly chopped
- 125g (4.5oz) spinach leaves
- Basmati rice, to serve

1 Place the curry paste, squash, basil and coconut milk into the slow cooker. Cook for 1.5 hrs on high (1 hr if chunks of squash are small).
2 Add in the frozen prawns and cook for a further 20 mins until cooked through and piping hot. Add in the spinach and mix. Cook for 5 mins.
3 Serve with basmati rice.

"You don't have to use balti paste. Make it sweeter with a tikka paste instead"

108 The Ultimate Slow Cooker Cookbook

MAIN MEALS

Cook's Tip
There's no need to defrost frozen prawns. Add them straight to the sauce and simmer until cooked and piping hot.

MAIN MEALS

MAIN MEALS

Cod, chorizo and butter beans one-pan

Comforting, quick and utterly delicious. The spicy oils from the chorizo in this dish add a lovely warmth and help to keep the fish moist

Serves 4 • Ready in 2 hrs

- 75g (2.5oz) diced chorizo
- 2 large garlic cloves, finely sliced
- 1tsp smoked paprika
- 400g (14oz) butter beans, drained and rinsed
- 250ml (9fl oz) white wine
- 4 x 150g (5oz) pollock or cod fillets

To serve:
- 2tbsp olive oil

1 Add all of the ingredients to the slow cooker, making sure to push down the fish. Cover and cook on high for 2 hrs until the fish is cooked through.
2 Transfer from the slow cooker on to plates using a slotted spoon as there is more poaching liquid than needed.
3 Drizzle with olive oil to serve, if liked.

Cook's Tip
We love pollock in this dish but hake is just as good an option. Make friends with your fishmonger!

"Chickpeas can be used instead of butterbeans for this filling dish"

MAIN MEALS

French moules marinière

These go beautifully with frites, or a lovely wedge of crusty bread

Serves 2 • Ready in 40 mins

- 600g (21oz) fresh live mussels
- 1 shallot, finely chopped
- 1 garlic clove, finely chopped
- 125ml (4.5fl oz) dry white wine
- 2tbsp butter
- 2tbsp flat-leaf parsley, chopped

1 Put the mussels into a colander and rinse under cold running water. De-beard any that need it by pulling away the fibrous membrane attached. Scrub off any attached barnacles. Discard any mussels that do not close when tapped. Rinse again.
2 Heat the slow cooker. Add butter until melted and mix in garlic and shallot.
3 Add the remaining ingredients, except the parsley, and stir to combine. Cover and cook for 40 mins.
4 Once the shells are open, put the mussels into 2 bowls with the cooking liquid. Serve scattered with parsley. Discard any closed mussels that cannot be opened easily.

Cook's Tip
Place the live mussels in a large bowl of cold water with 1tbsp of flour – they will purge any sand in their shells.

MAIN MEALS

Salmon Provençale with freekeh

Research has shown that omega-3 rich fatty fish such as salmon has a strong relationship with mental health

Serves 4 • Ready in 1-2 hrs

- 4 x 100g (3.5oz) pieces salmon fillet
- 250g (9oz) mixed tomatoes, larger ones quartered
- 2 garlic cloves, sliced
- 50g (2oz) mixed pitted olives
- 12 caper berries
- 1 lemon, sliced plus the juice of 1 lemon
- 100ml (3.5fl oz) dry white wine
- 2 x 250g (9oz) pouches cooked freekeh
- Large handful mixed fresh herbs (parsley, coriander and basil), finely chopped

You will need:
- Baking paper

1 Cut four 22cm (8.5in) circles of baking paper. Place a piece of salmon on one half of each circle. Add tomatoes, garlic, olives and caper berries, season and top with lemon slices.
2 Fold and twist edges of each circle to seal. Place in slow cooker and pour wine into each parcel before sealing completely. Place the lid on, and cook for 2 hrs on low, or 1 hr on high.
3 Heat freekeh following pack instructions. Add herbs and lemon juice and stir. Serve with the salmon.

MAIN MEALS

MAIN MEALS

Venison and butternut squash stew

This recipe is made with protein-packed venison and antioxidant-rich squash. If you can't find venison, you could use good quality, tenderised pork instead

Serves 6 • Ready in 4-5 hrs

- 4tbsp oil
- 700g (1.5lb) casserole venison, cubed
- 1tsp allspice
- 300ml (10fl oz) red wine
- 4 bay leaves
- 100g (3.5oz) butter
- 4 large shallots, sliced
- 3 carrots, sliced
- 2tbsp plain flour
- 1 butternut squash, deseeded and chopped, but not peeled
- Zest and juice of 1 orange
- 500ml (18 fl oz) beef stock
- 100g (3.5oz) fresh breadcrumbs
- 4tbsp chopped flat-leaf parsley

1 Heat half the oil in a frying pan, then brown the venison in batches. Set aside to cool, then put in a lidded plastic container, add the allspice, wine, and bay leaves, and leave in the fridge to marinate overnight.
2 The next day, heat the remaining oil and half the butter in a large pan and add the shallots and carrots. Cook for a few mins, add the flour and stir well. Gradually add the marinade, stirring continuously, then the venison, squash, orange zest and juice, and beef stock. Pour into slow cooker and cook for 4-5 hrs, until the meat is very tender.
3 For the topping, melt the remaining butter in a pan, add the breadcrumbs and stir for 5 mins, until browned. Remove from the heat, add the parsley and a pinch of salt, and scatter over the stew. Serve with basmati rice, if you like.

Cook's Tip
Prepare up to step 4, then cool and freeze. Defrost and continue with step 5 to make the pies.

Creamy cider rabbit stew

Rabbit might not be your first choice but most mainstream supermarkets sell it. Otherwise pick some up from your local butcher

Serves 4 • Ready in 5 hrs 30 mins

- 60g (2.5oz) butter
- 500g (1lb) rabbit fillet
- 200g (7oz) lardons
- 300g (10.5oz) shallots, peeled
- 1 onion, chopped
- 2 celery sticks, chopped
- 250g (9oz) parsnips, chunks
- 300ml (10.5fl oz) dry cider
- 300ml (10.5fl oz) chicken stock
- 6tbsp half-fat crème fraîche
- 2tbsp cornflour mixed with 2tbsp water
- 2tbsp Dijon mustard
- 2tbsp tarragon

For the pastry rounds:
- 225g puff pastry sheet, defrosted if frozen
- 1 egg, beaten to glaze

1 Heat half the butter in a large frying pan, add the rabbit, season and fry for 10 mins. Remove and set aside. Fry the lardons for a few mins until crisp, then set aside. Add the remaining butter to the casserole with the shallots, onion and celery, and cook for a few mins.
2 Add the parsnips, cider and chicken stock, along with the rest of the ingredients to the slow cooker. Cover and cook for 5 hrs.
3 For the pastry puffs, unroll the pastry and stamp out 8 x 5cm (2in) rounds. Place them onto a greased baking tray and score the tops with a sharp knife. Chill for 5 mins. Increase the oven temperature to 220°C/ 425°F/Gas 7.
4 Brush the pastry rounds with egg. Cook for 10 mins until golden brown.
5 Add the crème fraîche, cornflour mixture, mustard and tarragon to the stew. Warm through and stir until thickened. Serve the stew topped with their puff pastry "hats".

MAIN MEALS

Crispy duck cassoulet

For a little extra indulgence, serve with hunks of freshly baked, crusty bread to mop up all the juices with

Serves 6 • Ready in 2 hrs

- 200g (7oz) smoked lardons
- 300g (10.5oz) sausage, sliced
- 2tbsp duck fat or olive oil
- 2 shallots, finely diced
- 1 stick celery, diced
- 1 carrot, diced
- 1 bouquet garni
- 2 garlic cloves, crushed
- 400g (14oz) dried haricot beans, soaked overnight
- 6 confit duck legs
- Crusty bread, to serve

1 In a large frying pan fry the lardons for 5 mins, until browned. Add the sausage and fry for a couple more mins. Add the duck fat, shallots, celery, carrot, bouquet garni and garlic. Fry for a couple more mins until slightly softened.
2 Add the beans, along with 2l (4pts) of water. Put in the slow cooker, and cook for 2 hrs on low, until everything is soft. Check halfway through and add more water if needed.
3 Meanwhile, cook the confit duck legs according to the pack instructions.
4 Serve the duck on top of the cassoulet, with bread on the side.

Cook's Tip
Freeze for up to 3 months. Just make sure it's fully cooled before you pop it in the freezer.

MAIN MEALS

DESSERTS

DESSERTS
& BAKES

- 120 Guinness sticky toffee pudding
- 121 Poached pears with warm chocolate sauce
- 122 Cinnamon baked apples
- 122 Caramelised clementine risotto
- 123 Orange fairy cakes
- 124 Raspberry and coconut ice cream
- 125 Pineapple upside down cake
- 126 Banana bread
- 128 Change the mood chocolate pots
- 128 Brownies

DESSERTS

p121
Bake desserts like this in your slow cooker!

DESSERTS

Guinness sticky toffee pudding

Sticky toffee pudding is a British favourite, and with this slow-cooker recipe, it's never been easier!

Makes 8 • Ready in 3 hrs 30 mins

- 150g (5oz) butter, plus extra for greasing
- 150g (5oz) light muscovado sugar
- 2 large eggs
- 150g (5oz) self-raising flour
- ½tsp salt
- 1tsp vanilla extract
- 6 dates, pitted
- 200ml (7fl oz) Guinness
- 75g (3oz) golden syrup
- 75g (3oz) dark muscovado sugar

1 Grease a 3.5l (7pt) slow cooker basin. In a bowl, cream together the butter and sugar until light and fluffy using an electric whisk.
2 Add the eggs, flour, salt and vanilla, and whisk until well combined. Roughly chop the dates and stir through the mixture. Spoon into the slow cooker basin.
3 To make the sauce, gently heat the Guinness, golden syrup and sugar until the sugar has melted. Pour over the cake mixture, cover with a lid and cook on low for 3 hrs. The cake is cooked when an inserted skewer comes out clean.
4 Serve the cake on a lipped plate (to catch the toffee sauce) with plenty of hot custard.

DESSERTS

Poached pears with warm chocolate sauce

Also known as Poires belle Hélène, it's very simple to make and tastes utterly delicious

Serves 6 • Prep 10 mins • Cook 2 hrs 10 mins

- 6 firm dessert pears, such as Comice
- 350g (12oz) caster sugar
- 1 vanilla pod, halved
- 1 cinnamon stick
- 1 bay leaf
- Pared zest 1 lemon
- 750ml (1lb 10oz) vermouth rosé or bianco
- 170ml (6oz) double cream
- 200g (7oz) dark chocolate
- 50g (2oz) toasted hazelnuts, to scatter
- Ice cream or cream, to serve

1 Peel each pear, leaving the stalk in place. Cut out the core from the bottom, leaving a flat base so the pears stand up when served.
2 In a slow cooker, add the sugar, vanilla pod, cinnamon stick, bay leaf and lemon zest. Add the pears and pour over the vermouth.
3 Cook for 2 hrs on low, turning the pears over after an hour. Carefully remove the pears from the poaching liquid, reserving the syrup.
4 For the chocolate sauce, heat together the cream and chocolate in a small pan over a low heat, stirring until the chocolate has melted.
5 Stir in 3tbsp of the reserved sugar syrup until the sauce is glossy. Divide the pears between 6 serving dishes, drizzle the sauce over them and scatter with the toasted hazelnuts. Serve with ice cream or cream.

DESSERTS

Cinnamon baked apples

What could be simpler or quicker than having a baked apple for pud?

Serves 4 • Ready in 2 hrs 30 mins

- 4 large hard cooking apples, preferably Bramleys
- 50g (2oz) dairy-free spread or lactose-free butter
- 4tbsp demerara sugar
- 4tbsp raisins
- 80ml (3.5oz) water
- A pinch ground cinnamon

1 Using an apple corer, remove the core from the apples then score the circumference of the apple skin and place the apples into the slow cooker.
2 Divide the dairy-free spread or butter between the apples, stuffing it into each core cavity. Mix the sugar, raisins and cinnamon together and stuff the mixture into the cavities.
3 Pour the water around the apples and bake for about 2 hrs 30 mins or until the apples are tender.

Caramelised clementine risotto

You can use half a tin of condensed milk in this recipe

Serves 6 • Ready in 3 hrs 20 mins

For the caramelised clementines
- 6 clementines
- 100g (3.5oz) granulated sugar
- 2tbsp Grand Marnier or brandy

For the risotto
- 600ml (20fl oz) milk
- 2tbsp caster sugar
- 1 large knob of butter
- 175g (6oz) risotto rice
- 200ml (7fl oz) condensed milk, evaporated milk or cream

1 Pare and pith the clementines, keeping them whole and setting aside the peel.
2 Put the granulated sugar and 4tbsp water in a pan and heat gently, stirring until the sugar dissolves. Bring to the boil, then simmer over a medium heat for a few mins without stirring, until the syrup turns amber. Remove from the heat and dip the base of the pan briefly in cold water.
3 Stir in 4tbsp water, the Grand Marnier and a sliver of peel. Simmer gently for 10-15 mins. Add the clementines and cook for 2 mins, turn, then cook for another 2 mins. Take out with a slotted spoon and pour over the syrup.
4 For the risotto, grease the slow cooker pot with the butter. Add the milk, condensed milk, caster sugar, the pared rind from 2 clementines and the rice. Stir and cook for 3 hrs on low, stirring occasionally.
5 Spoon the risotto into dishes and top each with a clementine and a puddle of syrup.

DESSERTS

Orange fairy cakes

These individual cakes are infused with a fresh, citrus orange flavour, and are perfect for elevenses

Makes 8 • Ready in 1 hr, plus cooling

- 125g (4.5oz) gluten-free plain white flour
- 1 level tsp gluten-free baking powder
- 125g (4.5oz) dairy-free spread (we used Pure)
- 125g (4.5oz) caster sugar, plus 1 extra tbsp
- 2 eggs
- Grated rind and juice of 1 large orange

1 Put the flour, baking powder, spread, 90g (3.5oz) sugar and the eggs in a mixing bowl, and add half the orange rind and 1tbsp water. Beat well with a wooden spoon until mixed.
2 Put the paper (or silicone) cake cases into the slow cooker and spoon the batter into them.
3 Cover the slow cooker with a tea towel and place the lid on top. Bake for 1 hr on high.
4 Remove the cakes from the slow cooker and place on a wire rack to cool.
5 Heat the orange juice in a small pan on the hob with 1tbsp water and the extra 1tbsp sugar. Boil until syrupy. Pour over the hot fairy cakes, then sprinkle with the rest of the grated orange rind. Leave the fairy cakes to cool before serving.

DESSERTS

Raspberry and coconut ice cream

A vegan and naturally sweetened ice cream that's refreshing and light

Serves 4 • Ready in 1 hr, plus freezing

- 100g (3.5oz) pitted Medjool dates
- 250g (9oz) frozen raspberries
- 2 x 400ml (14fl oz) tins coconut milk, chilled overnight in the fridge
- 1tsp cornflour

1 Place the dates into the slow cooker and cover with 100ml (3.5fl oz) boiling water and cook on high for 1 hr.
2 Use a slotted spoon to remove the dates from the slow cooker and blitz with the raspberries, coconut milk, a pinch of salt and 2tbsp of the water mixed with the cornflour until smooth.
2 Place in a loaf tin. Cover with baking parchment and freeze overnight. Leave at room temperature for 5 mins before serving with fresh raspberries.

Cook's Tip
Try this recipe with the same quantity of another berry.

DESSERTS

> "Sprinkle the cake batter with nuts like pecans for extra crunch"

Pineapple upside down cake

Flip your cake making on its head by adding a bit of a tropical twist

Makes 8 • Prep time: 15 mins
Baking time: 3 hrs

- 170g (6oz) softened butter
- 170g (6oz) white sugar
- 170g (6oz) self-raising/cake flour
- 3 eggs
- Tin of pineapple rings in juice
- Glacé cherries
- 2tbsp brown sugar

1 Using a wooden spoon, beat the sugar and softened butter together until it begins to lighten in colour, and is fluffy. Using a large metal spoon, fold in the eggs and flour a little at a time until fully combined. Pour the juice from the tin of pineapple into your mix, and fold in until fully combined. You may need to add a few more spoonfuls of flour if the mix becomes too loose.
2 Grease the slow cooker pot with 1tbsp butter and line the bottom with a disc of baking paper. Whisk the melted butter and brown sugar together and pour it into the slow cooker pot. Then, arrange the pineapple rings in a pretty pattern. Pop a cherry in the centre of each ring and in any big gaps. Try to keep everything symmetrical.
3 Carefully pour over the cake mix, ensuring that you don't bash too much air out of it. Spread it gently so all of the pineapple is covered. Bake for 3 hrs on high or until golden and it has passed the cake skewer test.
4 Leave to cool for a couple of mins, then gently take out of the slow cocker. If you let the cake cool too much then the fruit will stick.
5 Serve warm with custard or ice cream, or leave to cool completely for a delicious afternoon snack.

DESSERTS

Banana Bread

A deliciously sweet dessert loaf that the whole family will love. Quick and easy and perfect for weekend baking

Serves 16 • Prep 20 mins • Cook 3 hrs

- 175g (6oz) self-raising flour
- 175g (6oz) butter or margarine
- 175g (6oz) caster sugar
- 3 eggs, beaten
- 3 ripe bananas
- 1tsp vanilla extract

1 Beat the butter and sugar together with a wooden spoon until it is light in colour and fluffy.
2 Then using a metal spoon, fold in the flour and eggs, a little bit at a time, until everything is well combined.
3 In a separate bowl, mash the three bananas into a paste with the vanilla extract, then gently add this in to your cake mixture. If you are concerned that the mix seems a little on the runny side, simply add in another handful or two of flour.
4 Line the slow cooker pot half way up with foil, then use a baking paper disc at the bottom. Tip the batter into the lined pot. Bake for 3 hrs on high until a knife comes out clean. Remove from slow cooker and cool before serving.

"Add a dash of all-spice, or a handful of chocolate chips to mix it up"

DESSERTS

Cook's Tip
Freeze brown bananas and then defrost them to use in this recipe.

DESSERTS

Cook's Tip
Replace 50ml (2fl oz) of the milk with coffee for a delicious and more energising result.

Change the mood chocolate pots

These go beyond mere silky chocolate goodness and can be adapted to whatever you need in terms of your mood

Makes 3 • Ready in 3 hrs 30 mins

- 150g (5oz) plant-based chocolate, finely chopped
- 1tbsp olive oil
- 150ml (5fl oz) plant-based milk
- 1tsp maple syrup, optional
- Coconut yoghurt, to serve

For the candied cacao nibs:
- 150g (5oz) cacao nibs, roasted
- 2tbsp maple syrup

For the cherry compote:
- 200g (7oz) fresh or frozen cherries
- 1tbsp maple syrup

1 Place the chocolate and oil in the slow cooker on low for 30 mins.
2 Add in the plant-milk (ideally at room temperature) and immediately whisk to combine. (Note: it may look like it's 'split' but keep mixing it until it forms a smooth consistency.) Add ¼tsp salt and taste; depending on your chocolate, you may like to add a teaspoon of maple syrup for sweetness. Carefully divide into 3 pots and place in the fridge for at least 3 hrs to set.
3 For the cherry compote, if you are using fresh cherries, halve and deseed each one. Add the cherries and maple syrup to the slow cooker and place on low for 1 hr.
4 To make the candied cacao nibs, combine roasted cacao nibs, maple syrup and a large pinch of salt in a small mixing bowl. Spread the mixture out on a baking tray. Bake for 30 mins until roasted and crispy.
5 Once the ganache is set and cacao nibs are cool, top the ganache with the cherry compote, a spoonful of coconut yoghurt and the candied cacao nibs, and enjoy.

Brownies

The ultimate dessert for chocolate lovers, at any time of day!

Serves 8-12 • Ready in 5 hrs

- 100g (3.5oz) 70% dark chocolate, broken into chunks
- 2 eggs
- 75g (3oz) golden caster sugar
- 75g (3oz) light muscovado sugar
- ½tsp instant coffee, dissolved in 1tbsp hot water
- 1tsp vanilla extract
- 90g (3.5oz) 0% fat Greek yoghurt
- 90g (3.5oz) plain flour
- ¼tsp baking powder
- 15g (0.5oz) cocoa powder
- Icing sugar, for dusting

1 Line the slow cooker with foil up halfway and a circle of baking paper on the bottom, then switch the slow cooker on to low.
2 Melt the chocolate and butter in a pan over a low heat or in the microwave; cool for 5 mins.
3 Whisk the eggs with the caster and muscovado sugars until light. Stir in the chocolate, then the coffee, vanilla and yoghurt. Sift over the flour, baking powder and cocoa powder, and gently fold together.
4 Pour the mixture into the slow cooker. Bake on low for 5 hrs. Leave to cool, then cut into slices and dust with icing sugar.

DESSERTS

The Ultimate SLOW COOKER COOKBOOK

Future PLC Quay House, The Ambury, Bath, BA1 1UA

Bookazine Editorial
Editor **Zara Gaspar**
Senior Designer **Phil Martin**
Senior Art Editor **Andy Downes**
Head of Art & Design **Greg Whitaker**
Editorial Director **Jon White**
Managing Director **Grainne McKenna**

Woman&Home Editorial
Group Editor **Hannah Fernando**
Creative Director **Phil Attaway**
Lifestyle Content Director **Charlotte Richards**
Group Food Director **Jen Bedloe**

Cover images
TI Archive - Chris Alack 2013

Photography
All copyrights and trademarks are recognised and respected

Advertising
Media packs are available on request
Commercial Director **Clare Dove**

International
Head of Print Licensing **Rachel Shaw**
licensing@futurenet.com
www.futurecontenthub.com

Circulation
Head of Newstrade **Tim Mathers**

Production
Head of Production **Mark Constance**
Production Project Manager **Matthew Eglinton**
Advertising Production Manager **Joanne Crosby**
Digital Editions Controller **Jason Hudson**
Production Managers **Keely Miller, Nola Cokely, Vivienne Calvert, Fran Twentyman**

Printed in the UK

Distributed by Marketforce, 5 Churchill Place, Canary Wharf, London, E14 5HU
www.marketforce.co.uk – For enquiries, please email: mfcommunications@futurenet.com

The Ultimate Slow Cooker Cookbook First Edition (LBZ5492)
© 2023 Future Publishing Limited

We are committed to only using magazine paper which is derived from responsibly managed, certified forestry and chlorine-free manufacture. The paper in this bookazine was sourced and produced from sustainable managed forests, conforming to strict environmental and socioeconomic standards.

All contents © 2023 Future Publishing Limited or published under licence. All rights reserved. No part of this magazine may be used, stored, transmitted or reproduced in any way without the prior written permission of the publisher. Future Publishing Limited (company number 2008885) is registered in England and Wales. Registered office: Quay House, The Ambury, Bath BA1 1UA. All information contained in this publication is for information only and is, as far as we are aware, correct at the time of going to press. Future cannot accept any responsibility for errors or inaccuracies in such information. You are advised to contact manufacturers and retailers directly with regard to the price of products/services referred to in this publication. Apps and websites mentioned in this publication are not under our control. We are not responsible for their contents or any other changes or updates to them. This magazine is fully independent and not affiliated in any way with the companies mentioned herein.

FUTURE
Connectors. Creators. Experience Makers.

Future plc is a public company quoted on the London Stock Exchange (symbol: FUTR)
www.futureplc.com

Chief Executive Officer **Jon Steinberg**
Non-Executive Chairman **Richard Huntingford**
Chief Financial and Strategy Officer **Penny Ladkin-Brand**
Tel +44 (0)1225 442 244